To Tom
Best
Wishes!

Starved Rock
Stories

Steve
Stout

Starved Rock
Stories
by
Steve Stout

Selected Histories and Images of North Central Illinois

Utica House Publishing Company
Utica, Illinois 61373

Library of Congress Catalog Card No. 96-90106
Stout, Steve
Starved Rock Stories
ISBN: 0-9609296-1-4

Dedicated
to my mother, **Eva Kathleen Neill Stout**,
who, with every birthday, gets younger and younger.

Manufactured in the United States of America.
First printing - October 1997

Utica House Publishing Company
Rural Route Number One
Utica, Illinois 61373

CONTENTS

Afternoon sunlight filters through the majestic Great Hall of **Starved Rock Lodge** outside Utica, Illinois. The log and stone lodge, built in the early 1930s by the Civilian Conservation Corps, is the heart of **Starved Rock State Park.** The popular Midwest recreation retreat plays host to hundreds of thousands of hikers and visitors every year.

THE CHOSEN GENERATION
CIRCA 1910
© *by Vivian Volk of La Salle, Illinois*

We are the chosen.

The cake, the frosting and
All the gooey goodness in between.
We have savoured it all—
Along with burnt edges,
Sour grapes and green apples.
We are the generation that remembers—
Trolley cars, coal heat, the iceman,
And hand-operated yesterdays.
We were born just before or
During the first WORLD WAR.
We bought Liberty bonds and
Sang, "the Yanks are Coming."
This great war spawned the golden egg.
We watched it crack and burst
And all its golden slime covered
a jazz-mad, speakeasy world.
When we dunked day old doughnuts
And buttered bread with daily despair.
We complacently rode
In a windblown rumble seat,
While the Jackass trampled
the Ivory—tusked gentlemen and
Buried him in the trenches.

To escape reality, we went fishing
With a willow pole, a can of worms
And a pony of 3.2.
Violently roused from our lethargy—
We suffered and survived another WAR.
Bigger, Bolder, Bloodier,
Which planted poison roots
Deep in every heart
We have watched eruptions of wealth,
Magic, medical miracles,
The creation of a robot world,
And learned the fear of an atomic holocaust.
We followed paths of instant transportation
And communication—
To worlds end and beyond—
We have viewed this fickle melodrama
Dancing like puppets
On power driven threads of hedonistic ambition.
We have raced this fantastic gamut
From grass roots to space—
While we swallow sweet-sour saliva
From an old fashioned lemon drop,
That keeps rolling—between tongue and cheek.

A small fishing boat glides quietly on the Illinois River passing **Starved Rock State Park**.

PROLOGUE

*T*he history of the Illinois Valley is essential to the diverse heritage of America in many different ways, but perhaps none as notable as the mission established at the native American village of Kaskaskia near Starved Rock. Founded by the French explorers Louis Joliet and Father Jacques Marquette in the late 1600s, the mission became the birthplace of Christianity in the Midwest wilderness and ultimately the center of a territory which grew to become the state of Illinois.

Father Marquette, dedicated to the cause of exploration as much as he was to his religion, braved many obstacles in his journeys that opened the heart of the new country. His name, among others, will live forever in the annuals of history as a man who relished the astonishment of discovery with little fear of the unknown. His sense of commitment was uniquely strong to both his country and his church. Even now, hundreds of years after his death, we owe him and the explorers who followed his path the continued preservation of their distinctive histories.

When I first moved to La Salle in 1974, I had little knowledge of Illinois Valley history. In the many years that I worked and studied in the area, I grew to admire the rich heritage of the community which had accepted me as a member.

From the many legends of the once strong tribes of area Native Americans to the construction of modern cities linked by rail, road, river and air, the Illinois Valley has evolved into a modern community important to the nation in numerous ways. The valley's history is layered with a wealth of significant events, both man-made and natural, which continue to influence the state and nation today.

Within the pages of this publication, certain local legends are retold and images, both new and old, are preserved in print. Oddly, I have little explanation as to why I picked these particular articles and photographs for this book. They merely represent a cross-section of the foundation which supports our daily lives at work and at home. Without question, there are definitely other important stories and sights which are missing from this collection. Perhaps they will be presented by future historians as a reminder of everything we owe the past, especially to study and remember the continuing evolution of our own backyard.

Steve Stout

September, 1997

The muddy dirt roads stand out in this year unknown image of the main street of **Utica**, Illinois.

THE FIRST GREAT DEBATE

T he year was 1858.

     On August 21, Ottawa, Illinois was broiling under the hot summer sun. Adding to the discomfort of its citizens were the choking dust clouds raised by hundreds of horse-drawn wagons and buggies that rolled into the village from all directions. By midmorning, the town was so deluged in dust that one newspaper reporter wrote that it resembled "a vast smokehouse." By noon, the crowds pouring into the public square created such chaos as was never seen before or since in the city.

     Although the estimates of the numbers varied, indications are that from 10,000 to 12,000 people were squeezed in and around the small park in the heart of Ottawa. In an almost carnival-like atmosphere, the crowds had come to listen to two popular Illinois politicians discuss the most sensitive and emotional issue of that era— slavery. Senate Republican candidate Abraham Lincoln would face off against popular incumbent Democrat Stephen A. Douglas in the first of seven debates. The nationally publicized discussions capsulized the issues which would throw the nation into civil war just three years later.

     The origin of the debates can be traced to Lincoln's own dark vision in the late 1850s of America's ominous future. Southern states were poised to revolt against the national government and the union was in desperate need of strong leadership. The prairie politician was haunted by the simple fact that slavery was morally reprehensible. That overpowering conviction led him to seek a national Senate position in order to help stop the spread of slavery to new territories applying for statehood.

On June 16, Lincoln accepted his party's acclamation to oppose Douglas with a very carefully prepared speech presented in Springfield. His opening sentences not only set the theme for the upcoming political battle, but he also prophesied a bloody war. Standing tall before party members in the Illinois Statehouse, Lincoln said: "If we could first know where we are and whither we are tending, we could better judge what to do and how to do it. We are now far into the fifth year since a policy was initiated, with the avowed object and confident promise of putting an end to slavery agitation. Under the operation of that policy, that agitation has not only ceased, but has constantly augmented. In my opinion it will not cease until a crisis shall have been reached and passed. A house divided against itself cannot stand. I believe this government cannot endure permanently, half slave and half free. I do not expect the Union to be dissolved— I do not expect the house to fall— but I do expect it will cease to be divided. It will become all one thing or all the other. Either the opponents of slavery will arrest the further spread of it and place it where the public mind shall rest in the belief that it is in course of ultimate extinction; or its advocates will push it forward till it shall become alike lawful in all the states, old as well as new, North as well as South."

Lincoln, in his eloquence, presented a point-by-point argument against the U.S. Supreme Court's 1857 Dred Scott decision, which declared that neither Congress nor local legislature could exclude slavery from new territories upon their admittance to the Union. He also voiced his opposition to the Kansas-Nebraska Bill, which had been introduced into the Senate by Douglas in 1854. The candidate maintained that both the decision and the legislation were simply silent subversions of the principles of liberty. His speech was a battle-call for true freedom for every American. He concluded, "We have to fight this battle upon principle, and principle alone!"

Soon afterward, in July, Douglas returned home from Washington where, after elaborate preparation,

> "A house divided against itself cannot stand."
> Abraham Lincoln

he began a summer of electioneering. Amid music, fireworks, banners and jubilation, his speeches were well received by the public and media alike as he stumped throughout the state. Lincoln followed on the incumbent's heels with campaign stops and speeches often at the same locations, but to somewhat smaller crowds. On more than one occasion, Lincoln was in the crowd to hear the Senator refer to him as "a kind, amiable and intelligent gentlemen, a good citizen and an honorable opponent." However, he also heard the "Little Giant" (as the Senator was nicknamed by his followers) warn his constituency that "Mr. Lincoln advocates boldly and clearly a war of sections, a war of the North against the South, of the free states against the slaves states— a war of extermination— to be continued relentlessly until the one or other shall be subdued, and all the states shall either become non-slave or become slave."

Lincoln and his Republican council, realizing that the campaign was not advancing to their advantage, formulated the idea of a series of public debates in the hopes of shaping a coalition of popular support. The single issue would be the extension of slavery in the United States and its territories. On July 24, the challenge was issued. Douglas, who had little to gain and much to lose, nevertheless was quick to accept his opponent's proposal. The format was soon arranged. The two candidates would face each other in the towns of Ottawa, Freeport, Jonesboro, Charleston, Galesburg, Quincy and Alton. The men agreed that they would alternately open and close the discussion at each location with set time limits.

Meanwhile, both of the politicians also scheduled independent speaking engagements in addition to the seven planned debates. To accommodate their pressing schedules, both Lincoln and Douglas often had to speak to several groups a day, travel in the midsummer heat and dust and frequently be on the road all night in order to make the necessary connections. Thus to the battle of intellectual prowess was added the further burden of sheer physical stamina.

It should be noted that the Ottawa debate was not the first time that Lincoln faced Douglas in a public forum. They had verbally battled each other in a highly publicized Springfield murder trial in 1838. Jacob M. Early, Lincoln's last army captain during his short stint in the Black Hawk War, had been killed during a violent argument with Henry B. Truett over mere politics. Truett had shot the man dead, allegedly in self-defense, as Early approached him with a chair over his head. Because the regular prosecutor was called as a witness in the case, Douglas was appointed prosecuting attorney. Lincoln, along with his other assisting attorneys, contended to the jury that Truett, who was a smaller man than Early, was acting in a reasonable manner because he believed that his life was in danger. Douglas argued Truett purposely was armed that night because he expected a fight and planned to kill Early. Lincoln's brilliant summation was considered largely responsible for the acquittal of the accused.

Despite the oppressive heat of the day and the seriousness of the issue to be debated, Ottawa harbored a carnival atmosphere on August 21, 1858. Area farmers left their work to see the two famous Illinois politicians, as did many shopkeepers and other area businessmen. Hawkers behind makeshift stands shouted slogans and attempted to sell their various wares to the crowds that pressed into the heart of the village. One visiting correspondent wrote: "National flags, mottos and devices fluttered and stared from every corner. Military companies and bands of music monopolized the thoroughfares around the Courthouse and the public square. Two brass twelve pounders banged away in the center of their city and drowned the hubbub of the multitude with their own high capacities for hubbub. Vanity Fair never boiled with madder enthusiasm." The New York Times reported that Illinois was the most important political battlefield in the entire country that summer.

Carrying hundreds of supporters from Chicago, a chartered train made a special stop at Morris to pick up Lincoln, who had spent the night there. The 17-car train had been promoted for weeks by Chicago newspapers, some of which declared the debate to be "the first grand encounter between slavery and freedom— Douglas and Lincoln." Arriving about noon in Ottawa, the special train was greeted by enthusiastic Republicans who escorted their candidate to the home of Mayor Joseph O. Glover. Lincoln later rode in a gaily decorated horse and carriage to the scene of the debate. (Ed. note: That same carriage is now one of the prized possessions of the La Salle County Historical Society Museum in Utica.) Rails and a maul (a large hammer) were carried high by those marching in the parade to symbolize the hard labor their nominee had performed years before in central Illinois.

About the same time Lincoln was being welcomed by his followers, Democrats were gathering at nearby Buffalo Rock to hail their hero, Douglas, who was traveling east to Ottawa after an overnight stay as the guest of Capt. J. L. McCormick in Peru. The cheering Democrats, determined to outdo their opponents, loudly accompanied Douglas into Ottawa with a huge procession of wagons and horses, as if it were a circus parade. Douglas and his supporters were entertained at the Geiger House before they left for the square.

The carnival atmosphere prevailed in the heart of town as the candidates approached. The speakers' platform, which had been left unguarded in the square, was commandeered by members of the huge crowd looking for a space to sit. Even the makeshift roof above the wooden platform had been occupied by several agile young men who looked down at the crowd. Unfortunately, as one of the attending reporters later wrote: "Half a dozen clowns on the roof broke some of the boards and let them down on the heads of the reception committees!" When the debaters finally did arrive, it took nearly a half hour to clear the stand before the dignitaries could be seated.

While they waited, the two speakers had a moment to mingle with the crowd as it surged even closer to the stands. One account says that Lincoln muttered to some nearby audience members as he spotted his opponent, "Here comes Douglas... A little man in some respects but a mighty one in others." Sweating in the oppressive heat, the two candidates mounted the wooden rostrum. Among the local notables who shared the platform with

Stephen A. Douglas
(Photo courtesy of the Illinois State Historical Society)

15

the two politicians were Chief Shabbona (locally famed Indian leader who had saved many white settlers in La Salle County during the short-lived Black Hawk War); Ottawa Mayor Glover; O. C. Gray, B. C. Cook and Washington Bushnell, Ottawa attorneys; Arthur Lockwood, local merchant; William Reddick, wealthy Ottawan (whose huge home, now a public library and office/community center, stands opposite the northeast corner of the park); George Walker, merchant and first La Salle County Sheriff; Judge John V. A. Hoes (who was a relative of President Martin Van Buren); J. F. Nash, banker and Circuit Clerk; John Manley, hardware merchant; and William Cogswell, industrialist and longtime supporter of Douglas.

Loosening his black string tie, Lincoln removed his coat and handed it to Cook. With a slight smile, he spoke softly, "Hold this while I stone Douglas..." and sat down.

It was then, at nearly 2:30 p.m., that most of the sunburnt faces in the crowd got their first look at the office holder and office seeker. The two men were as much in contrast physically as they were politically. Douglas was short (five foot, one inch tall) and heavy-set; his hair was thick and dark with streaks of gray, and his neck sat squarely on his broad shoulders. While the Senator was elegantly dressed, Lincoln's clothes hung on his thin, tall frame like loose laundry on a line. Clean-shaven (he did not grow his famous beard until much later), Lincoln the challenger nodded to Douglas as he approached the front of the platform to open the debate. Reporters leaned forward, ready to record every word with a new writing system, the first form of shorthand. Their mission was to insure that both sides of the slavery debate be accurately recounted for the rest of the world to hear. Some of the scribes did such a good job that even the cheers, jeers and other side comments of crowd members were transcribed within the two speeches.

In his booming voice, Douglas began: "I appear before you today for the purpose of discussing the leading political topics which now agitate the public mind. By an arrangement between Mr. Lincoln and myself, we are present here today for the purpose of having a joint discussion as the representatives of the two great political parties of the state and Union, upon the principles in issue between these parties and this vast concourse of people, shows the deep feeling which pervades the public mind in regard to the questions dividing us..."

With the crowd alternately cheering for and laughing with their Democratic hero, Douglas went on with his introduction and soon, he began to read from his opponent's own nomination speech. Lincoln supporters cheered the words. Douglas smiled and responded, "I am delighted to hear you Black Republicans say, 'Good!' I have no doubt that doctrine expresses your sentiments and I will prove to you now, if you will listen to me, that it is revolutionary and destructive of the existence of this government (members of the crowd screamed, "Hurrah for Douglas"). Mr. Lincoln, in the extract from which I have read, says that this government cannot endure permanently in the same condition in which it was made by its framers—divided into free and slave states. He says that it has existed for about seventy years thus divided, and yet he tells you that it cannot endure permanently on the same principles and in the same relative condition in which our fathers made it (more cheers)."

Looking out over the huge, sweating assembly, Douglas asked, "Why can it not exist into free and slave states? Washington, Jefferson, Franklin, Madison, Hamilton, Jay and the great men of that day, made this government into free states and slave states, and left each state perfectly free to do as it pleased on the subject of slavery ("Right, right!" came the shouts). Why can it not exist on the same principles on which our fathers made it ("It can, it can!")? They knew when they framed the Constitution that in a country as wide and broad as this, with such a variety of climate, production and interest, the people necessarily required different laws and regulations which would suit both the granite hills of New Hampshire and the rice plantations of South Carolina, ("Right, right!") and they, therefore, provided that each state should retain its own legislature, and its own sovereignty with the full and complete power to do as it pleased within its own limits, in all that was local and not national (loud applause). One of the reserved rights of the states was the right to regulate the relations between master and servant on the slavery issue. At the time the Constitution was formed, there were thirteen states in the union, twelve of which were slaveholding states and one a free state. Suppose this doctrine of uniformity preached by Mr. Lincoln, that the states should all be free or all be slave had prevailed and what would have been the result? Of course, the twelve slaveholding states would have overruled the one free state, and slavery would have been fastened by a constitution provision on every inch of the American Republic, instead of being left as our fathers wisely left it, to each state to decide for itself (more cheers). Here I assert that uniformity in the local laws and institutions of the different states is neither possible nor desirable. If uniformity had been adopted when the government was established, it must inevitably have been the uniformity of slavery everywhere, or else the uniformity of Negro citizenship and Negro equality everywhere.

"We are told by Lincoln that he is utterly opposed to the Dred Scott decision, and will not submit to it, for the reason that he says it deprives the Negro of the rights and privileges of citizenship (laughter and applause). That is the first and main reason which he assigns for this warfare on the Supreme Court of the United States and its decisions. I ask you, are you in favor of conferring upon the Negro the rights and privileges of citizenship ("No, no")? Do you desire to strike out of our state constitution that clause which keeps slaves and free Negroes out of the state, and allow the free Negroes to flow in and cover your prairies with black settlements ("Never")? Do you desire to turn this beautiful state in a free Negro colony ("No, no") in order that when Missouri abolishes slavery she can send 100,000 emancipated slaves into Illinois to become citizens and voters on an equality with yourselves ("Never, no")? If you desire Negro citizenship, if you desire to allow them to vote on an equality with yourselves and your rights, then support Mr. Lincoln and the Black Republican party who are in favor of the citizenship of the Negro ("Never, never").

"For one, I am opposed to Negro citizenship in any and every form (cheers). I believe this government was made on the white basis ("Good"). I believe it was made by white men for the benefit of white men and their posterity forever, and I am in favor of confining citizenship to white men, men of European birth and descent, instead of conferring it upon Negroes, Indians and other inferior races ("Good for you... Douglas forever").

The speaker then read from a list of resolutions which he claimed originated from a Republican meeting at Springfield four years earlier. Stressing the most radical points of the document, Douglas tied Lincoln to the advocation of the unconditional repeal of the Fugitive Slave Law, prohibition of the slave trade between the states and opposition to the acquisition of any more territory unless slavery was prohibited. He implied that these controversial statements represented the views of Lincoln and the state's Republican party. (This particular portion of Douglas' speech was later proved completely false. Neither Lincoln nor Republican leaders had ever endorsed these radical resolutions that were eventually traced to a "People's"

Convention held in Aurora during 1854.)

Douglas went on to associate Lincoln with the views of abolitionists and stated his claim "the Almighty never intended the Negro to be the equal of the white man." He did admit that this view did not mean that all black persons were meant to be slaves. He said that the race should be granted all the rights and privileges "consistent with the public good." He did not elaborate on that point, stating only that individual state legislatures should determine the social status of their Black population.

He concluded his statement by urging again that the states and territories be allowed to settle the slavery issue for themselves, a view consistent with the very principles he supported in local, state and federal government legislation during the 1850s. Some of his last words to the crowd were : "I believe that this new doctrine preached by Mr. Lincoln and his party will dissolve the Union if it succeeds! They are trying to array all the Northern states in one body against the South, to excite a sectional war between the free states and the slave states in order that the one or the other be driven to the wall!" He then turned and surrendered the stage to his opponent.

Lincoln rose slowly from his chair to wild applause that lasted several minutes before he could make himself be heard that afternoon. "My fellow citizens," he began, "when a man hears himself somewhat misrepresented, it provokes him... at least, I find it so with myself; but when the misrepresentation becomes very gross and palpable, it is more apt to amuse him (cheers and laughter)." He went on in this introduction presenting point-by-point denials of each charge that Douglas had leveled against him and his political party.

He then attempted to prove to the assembly that he was not the abolitionist which Douglas had claimed. Lincoln read from a speech he had delivered downstate in Peoria four years earlier which focused on his belief that ultimate emancipation of the slave in America would have to be a gradual, continuous process. History has seemed to gloss over the fact that Lincoln did agree with Douglas that Negroes were inferior to white people in some respects; however, he did emphasize that "in the right to eat the bread, without the leave of anybody else, which his own hand earns, he is my equal and the equal of Judge Douglas and the equal of every living man (great applause)!"

Aware that his differences with Douglas on many points were not so profound, he turned to the question that he would push at throughout the campaign: Was slavery morally right or wrong?

Douglas' viewpoint was that he did not care whether slavery was accepted or rejected just as long as his principle of popular sovereignty was upheld. Lincoln felt this perspective circumvented the main issue that one man holding another in bondage was intolerable.

Abraham Lincoln
(Photo courtesy of the Illinois State Historical Society)

"What is popular sovereignty? Is it the right of the people to have slavery or not have it, as they see fit, in the territories? I will state— and I have an able man to watch me— my understanding is that popular sovereignty, as now applied to the question of slavery, does allow the people of a territory to have slavery if they want to, but does not allow them to have it if they do want it (applause and laughter)! I do not mean that if this vast concourse of people were in a territory of the United States, any one of them would be obliged to have a slave if he did not want one; but I do say that, as I understand the Dred Scott decision, if any one man wants slaves, all the rest have no way of keeping that one man from holding them.

"When I made my speech at Springfield, of which the Judge complains, and from which he quotes, I really was not thinking of the things which he ascribes to me at all. I had no thought in the world that I was doing anything to bring about a war between the free and slave states. I had no thought in the world that I was doing anything to bring about a political and social equality of the black and white races. It never occurred to me that

I was doing anything or favoring anything to reduce to a dead uniformity all the local institutions of the various states. But I must say, in all fairness to him, if he thinks I am doing something which lead to these bad results, it is none better that I did not mean it. It is just as fatal to the country, if I have any influence in producing it, whether I intend it or not. But can it be true, that placing this institution upon the original basis- the basis upon which our fathers placed it— can have any tendency to set the Northern and the Southern states at war with one another, or that it can have any tendency to make the people of Vermont raise sugar cane, because they raise it in Louisiana, or that it can compel the people of Illinois to cut pine logs on the Grand Prairie, where they will not grow, because they cut pine logs in Maine where they do grow (laughter)? The Judge says this is a new principle started in regard to this question. Does the Judge claim that he is working on the plan of the founders of government? I think he says in some of his speeches- indeed I have one here now- that he saw evidence of a policy to allow slavery south of a certain line, while north of it, it should be excluded and he saw an indisposition on the part of the country to stand upon that policy, and therefore, he set about studying the subject upon original principles, and upon original principles he got up the Nebraska bill! I am fighting it upon these 'original principals'— fighting it in the Jeffersonian, Washingtonian and Madisonian fashion (laughter and applause)!"

Lincoln attacked Douglas as being a party of a conspiracy to insure that slavery would become a national institution. The candidate wondered why the word 'state' had been included in a sentence of the Kansas-Nebraska Act which read "it being the true intent and meaning of this bill not to legislate slavery into any territory of state." Since the Supreme Court had later allowed slavery into the new territories, he suggested that Douglas was laying the groundwork for another court decision which could make slavery legal in every state.

Lincoln then quoted from his "beau ideal of a statesman", Henry Clay, who once spoke of a class of men who would repress all tendencies to liberty and ultimate emancipation by "blowing out the moral lights around us..."

He closed by stating, "To my thinking, Judge Douglas is, by his example and vast influence, doing that very thing in this community, when he says that the Negro has nothing in the Declaration of Independence.

Henry Clay plainly understood that contrary notion. Judge Douglas is going back to the era of our Revolution and, to the extent of his ability, muzzling the cannon which thunders its annual joyous return. When he invites any people willing to have slavery, to establish it, he is blowing out the moral candles around us (cheers). When he says he 'cares not whether slavery is voted down or voted up,'... He is, in my judgement, penetrating the human soul and eradicating the light of reason and the lover of liberty in this American people (more cheers). And now I will only say that when, by all these means and appliances, Judge Douglas shall succeed in bringing public sentiment to an exact accordance with his own views, when they shall come to repeat his views and to avow his principles, and to say all that he says on these mighty questions— then it needs only the formality of the second Dred Scott decision, which he endorses in advance, to make slavery alike in all the states— old as well as new, North as well as South."

Nodding to his opponent on the podium behind him, Lincoln said, "My friends, that ends the chapter. The judge can take his half-hour." He moved away from the front of the stage.

Douglas' rejoinder was basically a shorter version of his opening statement. The Judge chided his opponent for failing to answer the charges that he originally addressed, hinting that Lincoln was silent due to the radical principles of his party.

At one point, members of the crowd shouted at Douglas, interrupting his speech. Mayor Glover moved to the front of the stand and pleaded, "I hope no Republican will interrupt Mr. Douglas... as respectable men we ought to hear Mr. Douglas, and without interruption." Resuming, Douglas pounded away at Lincoln until the tall man himself rose, moved forward and angrily interjected short comments on three different occasions. Two of the Republican committee men there grabbed Lincoln and, by a sudden jerk backwards, caused him to retreat from the front of the stand. One of the men reportedly commented, "What are you making such a fuss for... Douglas didn't interrupt you... Can't you see that the people don't like it?"

Unbothered, Douglas continued and ended his address by denying he was part of any conspiracy to make slavery a national institution. He reminded the audience that Lincoln truly believed that the Union cannot exist divided into free and slave states. "If it cannot endure thus divided, then he must strive to make them all free or all slave, which will inevitably bring about a dissolution of the Union!"

Pandemonium broke out the moment the debate ended. Several stout men rushed to the platform where they hoisted both candidates to their shoulders and carried them off to separate "victory" celebrations. Henry Villard, a witness to the debates, later observed, "It was really a ludicrous sight to see that grotesque figure (Lincoln) holding frantically on to the heads of his supporters." He added that Lincoln's legs were "dangling from their shoulders, and his pantaloons pulled up so as to expose his underwear almost to his knees!" Some other beefy Douglas supporters stumbled and dropped the man onto the ground. Picking themselves and their candidate up, the Democrats in the crowd continued their celebration through the Ottawa streets.

The Republican and Democratic newspapers both claimed victory for their candidates in greatly exaggerated front page accounts of the confrontation. Perhaps the cruelest report against Douglas appeared in the Ottawa Weekly Times on August 28, 1858 which stated, "It is said that he presented an appearance comical and novel, and more like a baboon on the front wagon of a menagerie train than like a Senator!" In contrast, The Illinois State Register concluded that "Lincoln withered before the bold, lucid and eloquent argumentation, and writhed under the sharp invective of Douglas."

History would record that the complex slavery issues discussed in that first and the other six debates across Illinois would ultimately fix the fate for both Lincoln and Douglas. By simple tabulations, Douglas would appear to have been the winner in the 1858 campaign confrontations for he retained his seat in Congress. However, the widely publicized debates pushed Lincoln into a position of national prominence and when the two mighty Illinois political opponents faced off in yet another election— this time for the Presidency in 1860— the outcome was to be quite different.

Throughout his political career and up to his assassination in 1865, Abraham Lincoln was to never forget his first verbal duel on that hot afternoon in Ottawa. In a letter to a friend, the famous statesman wrote: "Douglas and I, for the first time this canvass, crossed swords here (Ottawa) yesterday, the fire flew some, and I am glad to know I am yet alive!"

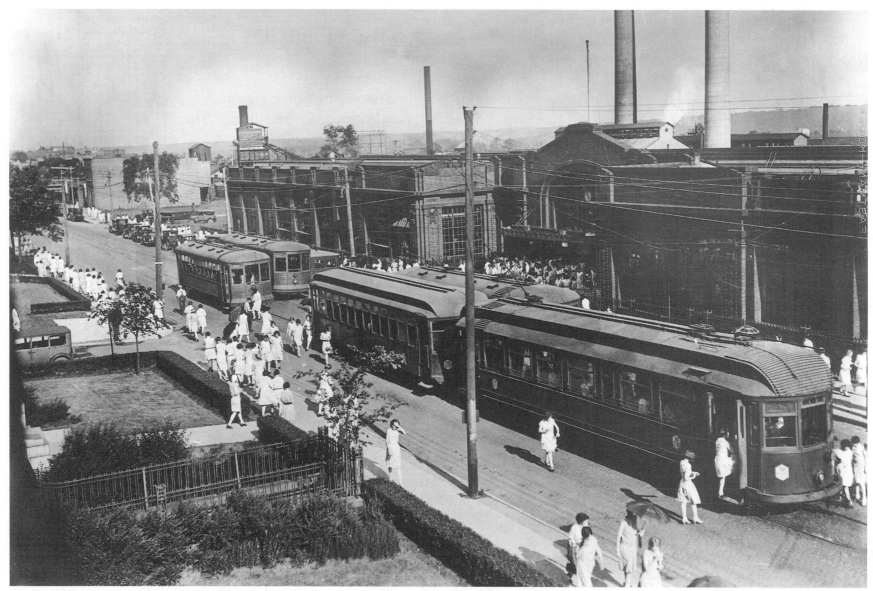

At the height of their popularity in the 1920s, electric train cars transported many thousands of **Westclox** employees to the front doors of the busy clock-making **Peru** plant. The **Interurban** served the entire **Illinois Valley** from **Princeton** to **Joliet**, providing both passenger and freight service until the automobile became commonplace.

Once the workplace of many thousands, the lights of the internationally recognized **Westclox** plant in **Peru** were turned off in the summer of 1980. The final layoffs closed a 90-year chapter within the **Illinois Valley's** diverse industrial history.

A winter's brilliant sunrise casts long shadows across a fresh carpet of snow over a **Starved Rock State Park** log cabin.

TRAGEDY IN NOVEMBER

The year was 1909.

Thomas P. Kenny, captain of Chicago Fire Engine Company 40, remembered the call: "On Tuesday, the 16th (of November) I got a call over the private wire from Chief Horan of the fire department in which he informed me that he had been requested to send firemen to Cherry, Illinois to aid in quelling the fire which was consuming the mine. Of my men, there was not one who had ever been inside a coal mine."

Kenny and his crew, though admittedly ignorant of coal mines, were not altogether unfamiliar with the fire problem in Cherry that week. Headlines in Chicago newspapers and other publications throughout the nation screamed out the story: "Hundreds feared lost in Cherry Mining Disaster!"

The village of Cherry lies in eastern Bureau County approximately 100 miles southwest of Chicago. When mining experts arrived there in 1905 to sink a vertical shaft into the prairie,[1] they had no inkling that four years later the mine would be the site of one of the worst disasters in United States mining history. As a result of a fire on November 13, 1909, 259 miners, some of them young boys in their teens, lost their lives.

The mine was opened by the St. Paul Coal Company, a main supplier of fuel for the Chicago, Milwaukee, and St. Paul Railway. The company at Cherry was linked by a spur track from Ladd, another mining town three miles away. In time, Cherry attracted numerous immigrant families, many of whom had little knowledge of the English language. The town became a melting pot of nationalities, including Italians, Slavs, Austrians, Lithuanians, Germans, French, Swedes, Poles, English, Belgians, Russians, Irish, Greeks, and Welsh.[2] Some of the houses at Cherry were built by the coal company on mine property; others were built by private owners. A plan of differential construction gave Cherry a unique appearance. With the exception of 35 houses in one row, no two houses of the same type stood side by side.[3]

In its first year of operations, the St. Paul mine was proclaimed "first class" by the district state inspector of mines. By its second year, Cherry had established itself as one of the most successful of the eight shipping mines in Bureau County. Although it ranked seventh in number of employees (353), it had the highest average number of days of operation (271) and ranked second in total output. The workers considered the mine a good one because it was well-equipped and the coal was easily mined. And because most of the coal went directly into the coal-fired locomotives of the Chicago, Milwaukee and St. Paul, there was no slack season in production.[4]

Warren R. Roberts, contractor and consulting engineer who constructed the 90-foot high steel tipple, called it the "safest mine in the world."[5] As investigation later proved, it was not the physical plant that was ultimately responsible for the disaster, but the questionable acts of the men in charge.

The first vein, dug deep into the flat plain in 1905, was found to have no real commercial value. Therefore the company burrowed deeper to reach a more rewarding second vein at 320 feet. Later, in August 1908, a third level was opened, which ran 165 feet below the second vein.[6] It was from the deepest vein that the highest quality of "black diamonds" was mined. Another major improvement in 1908 was construction of a huge ventilating fan 16 feet in diameter and more than six-feet wide. It ran at 180 revolutions per minute and circulated 180,000 cubic feet of air per minute.[7] By November 1909, Cherry miners were digging and hauling approximately 1,500 tons of coal to the surface each day.[8]

The miners worked in pairs, as was common in most Illinois coal operations of that era. Father-son and brother-brother teams were also very common. Wages were paid on a scale determined by the weight of coal dug by each team. Only the actual coal, not the rock and dirt that was dislodged and shoveled along with it, counted toward the miners' wages. Because the coal vein ran only 40 to 50 inches wide, much more of the worthless rock and shale were hauled up to the surface than coal. By 1909, each team averaged $1.08 a ton, with a good day being five tons for a team.[9]

Each team of miners dug from entries that shot off from a main tunnel. Miners on the second level used the "room and pillar" method, by which coal was taken from small rooms or chambers. Timber and natural pillars of earth served as supports for each room with thin curtains of canvas between the chambers to help cut down the choking dust created by the nearly constant digging. The third level of the mine, from which little coal had been extracted by the time of the disaster, was operated on the "long all" method, by which the workers dug across the length of the coal vein supported by timber shorings that lined the tunnel.[10] On each level there were also stables for the company's many mules. Mined coal was shoveled by miners into 6 x 3 foot wooden cars, which were then pushed by hand or hauled by mules along a series of tracks built into the floor. At the main shaft, the coal was recaged and eventually hoisted to the surface.[11]

In 1909, the St. Paul mine was operating on 7,217 acres at Cherry, of which 360 acres had been worked out. Company officials were W. W. Taylor, general manager; James Steele, mine superintendent; H. C. Maxwell, mine examiner; Alex Norberg, pit boss; John Bundy, mine manager; John Cowley, engineer for the main shaft; John Raisbeck, engineer for the escape shaft; and George Eddy, fire boss.[12]

Between 6:30 and 7 a.m. on Saturday, November 13, 1909, approximately 480 men and boys climbed into the shaky wooden cage that carried them into the dark pits. That day, as had been true throughout the previous few weeks, the shaft and tunnels were especially dark because the electrical system was out of order. The mine was instead illuminated with kerosene torches— two inches wide and 12 to 16 inches long, which were hung horizontally from the mine walls.[13]

About 12:30 p.m., shortly after the workers had finished lunch, mine manager Bundy ordered that six bales of hay be sent down to the mule stables; on that day there were approximately 40 mules laboring in the mine. When the car containing the hay reached the second level, it was pushed towards the stables by Robert Deans and 15-year-old Matt Francesco. As the car neared the stables, the miners gave it a final shove and watched it roll to a stop near the downward shaft. Turning away, they walked back to the main cage area.[14]

What the two men failed to see was that the dry hay, stacked high in the car, had stopped beneath one of the flaming torches, allowing oil to drip onto the bales. Some time later, sparks created a small fire inside the wooden car. The Cherry mine disaster had begun.

Workers raced to rebuild the destroyed fanhouse during the 1909 **Cherry** coal mine disaster. Smoke from the fire in tunnels several hundred feet below is seen pouring out of the main shaft. The official death toll from the tragedy was 259 men and boys lost.

According to testimony given weeks later at the inquest, initial efforts to extinguish the small blaze did not begin until after one o'clock and were very unorganized and unsuccessful. Tragically, because the miners were so accustomed to occasional fires, there was little concern given to the burning car. As was customary on Saturday, many miners took an early leave at 1:30, and those few who saw the fire assumed that it was under control. One man who passed the car on his way to the surface judged that the blaze could have been put out "easily" with the coats of the departing miners.[15]

Deans and Francesco were the first to spot the blaze, which they calmly reported about 1:25 to their immediate superior, Alex Rosenjack, who operated the cage lift between the second and third levels. Together, the men shoved the burning car back and forth along the mine floor, but instead of extinguishing the fire, they instead accidentally ignited the overhead timber supports. The men next tried to push the burning car through the main air shaft towards the sump near the mule barn, but the heat was too intense. Then they attempted to push the car onto the cage, thinking to lower it to the sump at the third level. In the process, however, the woodwork on the side of the cage caught fire. Before the car was secure in the cage, Rosenjack gave the signal to lower, and the car and hay tumbled under the cage and into the third level sump, where the fire was soon extinguished with the water hose used to service the mules. Nevertheless, the blaze continued to spread on the second level.

News of the fire traveled slowly through the mine, and little notice was given it by the working miners. Leaving their site would mean losing pay, and most therefore continued to dig.

Meanwhile, the increasing heat and smoke prevented Rosenjack, Deans and Francesco from connecting the third level hose, the only one in the entire mine, to a water pipe near the main cage. The pipe was too small, the water too hot, and the canvas hose could not be held against the opening of the pipe.[16]

When the deadly seriousness of the fire became apparent, several mule drivers and company men attempted to warn the diggers. The first cry of "Abandon the mine!" did not come until a full 45 minutes after the blaze was first discovered. Exits soon became blocked and the smoke began to form black damp- the toxic gas created from coal burning in an atmosphere lacking sufficient oxygen. The blaze spread until the escape hatch was engulfed in flames, leaving only the main shaft clear.

On the surface, rescue efforts were formed quickly by local citizens who rushed to the company yard at the blaring of the mine's emergency whistle. The number of frightened people around the company's mammoth tipple soon grew into the hundreds.

Mine manager John Bundy, with the help of pit boss Alex Norberg, formed a rescue crew and made several trips down the already smoking main shaft to save choking miners who were on the brink of death.[17]

Sixteen-year-old Peter Donna and his father, John, were among the miners trapped on the bottom level. The first hints of danger were small puffs of smoke coming from under the curtain of the entry. The two men escaped by scrambling up the 10-foot ladder to the second level. Peter Donna related his story before his death in 1977 at the age of 84:

After my father and I got to the second level...the fire blocked us off. It singed the hair on the side of my face and head.

We circled around the burning section and made our way to the main lift. The smoke almost overtook us. I led the way with one foot on the bottom floor railing... All the lights were out and our match wouldn't stay lit. We met only a few others who came with us on the way.

When we finally reached the lift, there was no trouble getting on it and up the shaft. It took several seconds for my eyes to get adjusted to the bright light of the surface and when I finally could see, I couldn't find my father.

I wanted to go back down into the mine and get him, but they stopped me. After a couple more cage-loads of men came up, my father stepped off with an old man he had saved.[18]

John and Peter Donna's luck was indeed strong, for almost immediately after they escaped, the ladder upon which they had climbed to safety was ablaze. The remaining miners, now trapped, ran back into the far reaches of the tunnels.

On the surface, an idea came to Norberg. The huge fan that blew air into the deep tunnels was still in operation, and was feeding fresh oxygen to the flames. Running to the signal, Norberg rang the bell seven times, ordering the fan stopped. What he did not realize was that the fan was also giving air to the desperate miners below. Bundy countered the order by signaling that the fan be reversed, thus pulling the fire away from the main shaft. It seemed to be a good idea, but soon the fan house itself was consumed by the red flames, cutting off any escape from the shaft.

The miners could be saved only if strong men with fresh air in their lungs would join the rescue attempt. "My God, boys, we need help!" Bundy pleaded with the crowd. "Who is willing to risk it for the sake of the boys down below?"

Several stepped out of the near-hysterical crowd and volunteered to make the perilous descent. Bundy picked those he thought to be the strongest and, with Norberg, again walked onto the cage. Many lives would depend on the bell signals, which informed the engineer to raise, lower, or stop the lift.

Two women made widows by the mine disaster walk back into the village from the **Cherry** coal company's yard.

The following men prepared to descend: John Bundy, mine manager; Alex Norberg, pit boss; Andrew McLuckie, miner; Dominic Formento, grocer; John Sczabrinski, cager; Joseph Robesa, driver; James Spiers, miner; Mike Suhe, miner; John Flood, clothier; Robert Clark, miner; Isaac Lewis, liveryman; and Harry Stewart, miner. With their eyes fixed on the crowd staring back at them, the men disappeared into the shaft, which by then was smoking heavily.

Six times the heroes entered into the smoky hole, returning helpless victims from certain dark death to the bright surface. The rescuers themselves were burned and nearly overcome with smoke with each descent but continued their effort. During the seventh trip, a meaningless jumble of clangs sounded sharply from the signal bell. "My God, boys," John Cowley gasped, "Those signals don't mean anything!" The crowd screamed at him to pull up the cage. Remembering the commands from Norberg, the engineer refused. He would wait for a recognizable signal. The bell continued to ring meaningless throughout the steam engine house. Confused by the people surrounding him who screamed to pull the rescuers up, Cowley threw into motion the clutch controlling the cage. The huge wheels slowly began to wind up the steel cables that rose out from the smoking hole. The enraged, fearful and hysterical friends and families pushed closer to the pit. The town's fear turned to instant grief as the cage appeared through the smoke. The entire cage and its contents were on fire. Mouths dropped open and faces in the assembly drained ghost white as shock overcame them. The 12 heroes had been hideously transformed into martyrs.[19]

Eight of the men were lying on the floor of the cage, twisted and tangled together. The bodies of the other four men were on top of the blackened pile as if they had been trying to scale the heavy cable to safety as the flames overcame them.[20] To add even more terror to the nightmare scene, many on the surface quickly realized that all hope for recovery of any workers still trapped in the mine was lost. The fire on the lift had closed the last exit.

> "My God, boys. Those signals don't mean anything!"
> John Cowley

At eight o'clock on the evening of the disaster, company officials ordered that the mine be sealed in order to smother the flames. Feelings ran high over that announcement, which seemed to doom any of those still alive in the veins. Stories circulated through the town that mine officials were attempting to save the company works, at the expense of the miners' lives.[21]

Cherry Mayor Charles Connolly deputized extra marshals as thousands of sightseers converged from surrounding communities.[22] All 19 saloons in the area were ordered closed.[23]

Charitable agencies gathered immediately to aid the suffering widows and orphans. The Red Cross, Knights of Pythias, and area churches organized relief committees.[24] The Chicago Tribune sent a trainload of special medical supplies and personnel while the coal company itself opened its local store to insure that no one went hungry during the tragedy's aftermath. The coordinating body for those efforts, known as the Cherry Relief Committee, was composed of Ernest P. Bicknell, national director of the American Red Cross; Duncan McDonald, president of the United Mine Workers of Illinois; James Hanney, local president of the Cherry UMW; Sherman C. Kingsley, superintendent of the United Charities of Chicago; Patrick Carr, member of the state board of the Illinois UMW; and Mayor Connolly.[25]

By Sunday morning, Robert Y. Williams and other engineers from the Mine Explosion and Mine

Rescue Station of University of Illinois arrived with oxygen helmets, resuscitation apparatus, and special rescue equipment. Their efforts were augmented by the assistance of similar teams from Ohio, Iowa, Missouri, and as far away as Pennsylvania.[26]

> "I did not fear the flames... I feared the terrible and fatal black damp..."
> Thomas P. Kenny

Protected by oddly-shaped oxygen helmets, two men descended successfully to the second vein through the air shaft. However, once there, they found that could do little to search for survivors due to the tremendous heat and thick smoke. The men were returned to the surface and the shaft was once again covered. Another attempt was made on Monday, November 15, but the smoke and steam were too dense for rescue work.[27]

Unknown to those on the surface, several miners had survived the initial fire and smoke by burrowing deep into a cavern in the far reaches of the second vein. Working many hours together, they barricaded themselves from the deadly black damp with a wall of timbers and wet dirt. Led by George Eddy, assistant mine manager, and Walter Waite, mine examiner, the group discovered a small pool of water beneath the coal seam, which became their only food. "If we had not found that seam of water," Waite later said, "we could not have lived two days." Darkness fell hard over the men, and the pain of hunger, as well as the stifling heat and contaminated air, drove some to delirium.[28]

Above ground, the people of Cherry were demanding that rescue efforts be resumed. Desperate threats were also made against St. Paul Coal Company officials. Bureau County Sheriff O. H. Skoglund reported that he had discovered a plot to blow up the sleeping cars of company representatives. Skoglund requested protection from Illinois Governor Charles S. Deneen, who responded by calling out the state's National Guard. Cherry was not placed under martial law, but a tense atmosphere prevailed.[29] Sensing the wrath of the distressed villagers, miners Alex Rosenjack and Robert Deans left town on Monday in fear of their lives. It was later discovered that Deans had fled to Scotland and Rosenjack to nearby La Salle, where he remained until called to testify at the inquest.[30] John Cowley, the engineer who delayed in lifting the rescue cage containing the dozen martyrs, was placed under heavy guard in a closeby village; he, too, eventually moved from the area.[31]

For days after the original disaster, the mine works remained, in one observer's words, "a roaring furnace."[32] Mine officials, unable to control the fire with local reserves of water, shipped in supplies from the fire department at Ladd and soon decided that additional equipment and professional firefighters would be needed if they were to reenter the mine. A call was put out to the Chicago Fire Department.

"At 2:30 (on Tuesday, Nov. 16), just as if we had been called to fight a fire in the loop district of the city, we were at the depot and had boarded a train," Captain Kenny later recalled. "We took with us one engine and a truck. The men carried with them all their implements and their hard firefighting clothes. The special train consisted of two freight cars in front, one baggage car and one flat car, on which the engine and truck were loaded.

"I never in my life traveled so fast! We went over the Chicago, Burlington & Quincy Railroad to Mendota. The distance is 83 miles and we made it in 62 minutes, more than a mile a minute! There was another special engine that awaited us and drew our train to Cherry. We immediately unloaded, but were unable to work that night.

"The next morning we conveyed the engine to the pond nearby and laid out a lead of hose to the main shaft. I went to the mine officials and asked permission to set my men to work and go down into the shaft and begin at once the fighting of the fire, but they referred me to the mine experts and examiners who told me that it was folly to attempt to enter that mine as the flames were seething with terrible force... I pleaded with them, but they refused to unseal the shaft and allow my boys to go down."

Later in the week, the Chicago Fire Department provided five tank cars of water, each with a capacity of 10,000 gallons. Within minutes of unsealing the main shaft, tons of water were poured into the pit. On Thursday evening, November 18, firemen descended the main shaft and fought the blaze directly. The first battle against the deadly underground blaze lasted only two hours before the crew was forced to retreat back up the shaft. "I did not fear the flames..." Kenny told newspaper reporters, "I have been accustomed to such dangers all my life. I feared the terrible and fatal black damp, which is the terror of all miners."[33]

36

During the next 24 hours, Kenny and his men worked in relays underground until the greater part of the fire was extinguished. Kenny told the experts, "I firmly believed that if we could have reached the east side of the second vein we could have completely conquered the fire." This was impossible as it was buried in vast tonnage of debris and cave-ins."

The blackened bodies of four miners were discovered on Friday, nearly one week after the disaster had occurred. By Saturday, November 20, it appeared that the fire was under control and that cleanup crews could enter the mine safely.[34] Out of the crowd of spectators who poured into Cherry that week came a hero named David E. Powell, superintendent of a coal mine at Braceville. Racing to the disaster site after hearing news of the fire, Powell and several of his veteran co-workers stepped forward insisting access to the sealed pit to search out survivors. As all hope of any men alive below was then gone, initially the Braceville men were turned away. Later in the week, at Powell's continued strong insistence, his crew was lowered down the main shaft. The brave men fought their way through pockets of the deadly smoke and tunneled across tons of debris.

Meanwhile, the group of miners trapped below in their barricaded chamber had no way to keep track of the passing time. Some were certain that all rescue attempts had missed them. On that Saturday, one of the trapped miners, crazed from eight days of confinement, tore down the barrier and raced out, fatally striking his head on the low mine roof. Four of the miners decided also to venture into the smoky passageway. They did not know if the killing black damp remained. As they crawled along the tunnel, they heard the sounds of Powell's team, who responded to their weak cries for help. In all, 21 miners were brought to the surface, their blackened heads covered with canvas to protect their eyes from the bright sunlight following their dark ordeal.[35]

The rescued miners were treated by a medical crew in nearby railcars and then carried home on horse-drawn wagons. The oldest member of the group, Daniel Holafcak, refused assistance and stumbled home alone: he died two days later—the 259th and final fatality of the disaster.[36]

Rescue efforts continued throughout the week, but the condition of the tunnels prevented access to all parts of the mine. Steam and smoke blocked the many passageways, and water accumulated in three and four-foot pools throughout the third level. On Wednesday, November 24, work crews discovered that many coal pillars were on fire, releasing a noxious gas. On the morning of the 25th, mine inspectors and coal company officials decided unanimously that both shafts would have to be sealed. Steel rails and concrete were used to close the openings.[37]

With the closing of the mine, there was no question that the lost miners were dead. The business of determining compensation for widows and children had to begin. Already, charges and countercharges were being made. Duncan McDonald reported that a

The pink mine dumps of the long-closed coal mine dwarfs the small village of **Cherry**, Illinois in this modern aerial view. The bulk of the worthless rock was dumped long after the disaster occurred. Lacking modern equipment, miners built the hills one hand shovel after another.

"county official and a representative of the coal company" were trying to arrange private settlements with the bereaved families; at the same time, unscrupulous attorneys were soliciting cases "on a fifty-fifty basis." Some families feared that they would receive no compensation at all because the company was entitled to declare bankruptcy.[38]

With the approval of the Cherry Relief Commission, an official mediator entered the discussion between mine representatives and company officials. That man was John E. Williams, a Streator businessman and onetime miner whose persistence and tireless research were responsible for the final settlement.

Williams suggested two alternatives: appointment of an arbitration committee by President William Howard Taft or settlement by the standards used in the English Workmen's Compensation Act of 1906. The latter plan was agreed upon, and pensions were determined by numbers of dependents, amount of service and average weekly salary.[39]

The settlement was administered by a new relief commission created in June 1920. McDonald and Bicknell again served; the new commissioners were E. T. Brent of the Coal Operators' Association of Illinois, Edwin Perry of the UMW and Williams, who also represented relief committees in Streator, La Salle, Peru and Oglesby. Former Lieutenant Governor Lawrence Y. Sherman was named chairman. The amount contributed by private groups and the St. Paul Coal Company was enough to give approximately $1,800 to every family whose breadwinner had been killed.[40]

The horror prompted Governor Deneen to call a special session of the Illinois General Assembly. Stronger regulations for both mine workers and owners were enacted. In state regulations of 1910 and 1911, new requirements were established for fire-fighting equipment in the mines and on the surface; certification tests were developed for hoisting engineers and other key workers. Funds were also appropriated for more mine rescue stations. Those measures were followed in 1911

A wreath is layed at the foot of the **Cherry Miners Memorial Cemetery** monument during the 75th anniversary observance held in 1984. The monument, erected by the United Mine Workers of America in 1910, is dedicated to the workers who perished in the coal mine fire.

by a liability act, which became the basis of the Illinois Workmen's Compensation Act.[41]

In the latter part of 1910, the St. Paul Coal Company reopened the Cherry mine and more than 250 men were hired. The company abandoned any further mining of the charred second vein. It developed instead the third vein, which the men worked until 1927. By that time, the Cherry mine, like many other northern coalfields, could no longer compete with the mechanized operations of southern Illinois in which the coal veins were closer to the surface.[42]

> "...the biggest bunch of carelessness I have ever seen."
> Peter Donna

Today, only the reddish slag piles stand like small mountains on the Illinois farmland to mark the location of the once busy Cherry mine. The giant tipple and the rest of the above-ground works have been removed, and the yard has been converted to farmland. Cherry itself was thought doomed to extinction after the mine closed, but the village now has a population of about 500 people, most of whom work outside the town.[43]

For years after the disaster, on each November 22, George Eddy held reunions for the disaster's survivors.[44] On the anniversary of the tragedy itself, November 13, citizens of Cherry paid homage to all the victims with a march from the mine site through the village to the Cherry Memorial Cemetery, where most of the dead are buried.[45] But as the memory of that day has passed with time, so did interest in the annual observances. The processions have long faded into history.

Peter Donna, one of the longest living survivors of the 1909 tragedy, repeated his harrowing story to anyone who asked to hear it, but fewer people asked as years passed. Donna never reentered the Cherry mine; he spent his years in occupations ranging from professional baseball player to grocery clerk and died on September 12, 1977. To that day, he called the disaster "the biggest bunch of carelessness I have ever seen."

FOOTNOTES

[1] The most complete accounts of the Cherry mine are found in the coal reports published annually by the Illinois Bureau of Labor Statistics, hereafter cited as Illinois Coal Report. See Illinois Coal Report, 1905, p. 208.

[2] Illinois Coal Report, 1910, p. 494.

[3] F. P. Buck, The Cherry Mine Disaster (Chicago: M.A. Donohue & Co., 1911), pp. 9,32.

[4] Illinois Coal Report, 1906, p. 183; Illinois Coal Report, 1907, pp. 194-95.

[5] Anton Demichelis, Memorial of the Fiftieth Anniversary of the Cherry Mine Disaster (Peru, Il.: St. Bede Abbey Press, 1959), p. 4; Illinois Coal Report, 1910, p.461; La Salle Daily Tribune, Nov. 15, 1909, p. 3, col. 4.

[6] Illinois Coal Report, 1909, p. 2101; The Cherry Mine Disaster; Report of Duncan McDonald, Seymour Stedman and the Executive Board of the United Mine Workers of Illinois (Chicago: Campbell Co., 1910), p. 13; Illinois Coal Report, 1910, p. 459.

[7] Illinois Coal Report, 1908, p. 203.

[8] Illinois Coal Report, 1910, p. 468.

[9] Ibid., p. 140; Illinois Coal Report, 1909, p.103; author's interview with Peter Donna, Lexington House Convalescent Center, Spring Valley, Il., Aug. 15, 1977 (hereafter cited as Donna Interview).

[10] Andrew Roy, A History of the Coal Miners of the United States (Columbus, Ohio: J. L. Trauger Printing Co., 1907), pp. 44'-42: Illinois Coal Report, 1905, p. 28; Illinois Coal Report, 1910, p. 468.

[11] Illinois Coal Report, 1909, p. 202; Illinois Coal Report, 1910, p. 469; Donna Interview.

[12] Illinois Coal Report, 1910, p. 468.

[13] Ibid., p. 469.

[14] Ibid., pp. 463-65

[15] Ibid., p. 460.

[16] Ibid., p. 469-72.

[17] Accounts of miners during the fire are taken from ibid., pp. 472-73; Buck, pp. 46-84; La Salle Daily Tribune, Nov. 15, 1909, p. 1, cols. 1 ff.

[18] *Donna Interview.*

[19] Cowley wrote a lengthy article about the tragedy titled "Death Cage Story;" see La Salle Daily Tribune, Nov. 18, 1909, p. 1, cols. 1 ff.

[20] Illinois Coal Report, 1910, pp. 472-73.

[21] Demichelis, p. 9; La Salle Daily Tribune, Nov. 15, 1909, p. 1, cols. 5 ff.

[22] La Salle Daily Tribune, Nov. 15, 1909, p. 4, col. 2.

[23] They were not allowed to resume business until Nov. 25, Streator Daily Free Press, Nov. 26, 1909, p. 3, cols. 1 ff.

[24] Ernest C. Bicknell, The Story of Cherry (Washington, D. C.; American Red Cross, 1911), pp. 7-8; Chicago Post, Nov. 15, 1909, p. 1, cols. 3-4; Chicago

Daily Tribune, Nov. 16, 1909, p. 2, cols. 4 ff.

[25] Chicago Daily Tribune, Nov. 15, 1909, p. 2, col. 7.

[26] Chicago Record-Herald, Nov. 16, 1909, p. 1, cols. 7 ff.; Chicago Daily Tribune, Nov. 16, 1909, p. 1, cols. 1 ff.; University of Illinois Register, 1909-1910 (Urbana: University of Illinois, 1909), p. 406; Illinois State Geological Survey Year-Book for 1909 (Urbana: University of Illinois, 1909), pp. 296-97.

[27] Illinois Coal Report, 1910, pp. 495-96.

[28] Those details were recorded on Walter Waite's diary, written during his imprisonment and reprinted in Bureau County Republican (Princeton), Nov. 25, 1909, p. 1, cols. 1 ff.

[29] Chicago Daily Tribune, Nov. 17, 1909, p. 1, cols. 7 ff.; Chicago Daily News, Nov. 17, 1909, p. 1, cols. 1 ff.

[30] Duncan McDonald, "The Cherry Mine Disaster," TS, pp. 4-5, Duncan McDonald Collection, Box 2, Folder 18, Illinois State Historical Society, Springfield; La Salle Daily News-Tribune, Nov. 16 (p. 4, col. 2), Nov. 17 (p. 1, cols. 1 ff.), 1909.

[31] Donna Interview.

[32] McDonald, p. 2.

[33] Chicago Daily Tribune, Nov. 16, 19098, p. 1, cols. 6 ff.; La Salle Daily Tribune, Nov. 17, 1909, p. 1, cols. 5 ff.; Demichelis, p. 10.

[34] Illinois Coal Report, 1910, pp. 495-97.

[35] Buck, pp.123-33; Bureau County Republican (Princeton), Nov. 25, 1909, p. 1, cols. 1 ff.

[36] Donna Interview; La Salle Daily Tribune, Nov. 23, 1909, p.2, col 1.

[37] Illinois Coal Report, 1910, pp. 496-97.

[38] McDonald, p. 4.

[39] Illinois Coal Report, 1910, pp. 503-26

[40] Bicknell, pp. 10-11.

[41] Earl R. Beckner, History of Labor legislation in Illinois (Chicago: U. of Chicago Press. 1929). pp. 300-01

[42] Illinois Coal Report, 1911, pp.236-37

[43] Illinois Blue Book, 1977-1978, p. 549.

[44] Bureau County Republican (Princeton), Nov. 24, 1910, p. 1, col. 1; Daily Free Press (Streator), Nov. 13, 1911, p. 1, cols. 1 ff.

[45] Demichelis, p. 16; Daily News-Tribune (La Salle), Nov. 13, 1959, p. 12, cols. 1 ff.

Shippingsport Bridge, the lift span which connects the cities of **La Salle** and **Oglesby**, raises its middle deck to allow a slow-moving paddlewheel boat to pass underneath. Completed in 1929, the aging structure has frustrated generations of motorists who curse the decrepit bridge as they line up and wait for passing tugboats and long barges.

Tens of thousands of area residents lined the brick main streets of **Peru** in the summer of 1935 to observe the city's **Centennial Celebration**. Similar parades and celebrations were held during the city's 150th birthday party in 1985.

La SALLE- LITTLE RENO OF ILLINOIS

The year was 1946.

Every night, the town was wild. Cars and couples packed the streets of the tiny city. Live band music filtered out past bright neon lights. Cards were dealt. Roulette wheels whirled. Throughout the county the arms of thousands of slot machines were wrestled up and down all night long. Money was won. More money was lost.

It was dubbed "Little Reno." It was La Salle, Illinois.

The origins of wagering in the Illinois Valley can most likely be traced back through history to the immigrants who had carved out the Illinois-Michigan Canal during the mid-1800s. The hard-working newcomers, for whom coming to America was a great risk in itself, would gamble a portion (or all) of their earnings on most anything. To compliment these laborer bettors, coal miners and riverboat crews, (the stereotype of which were also known to enjoy gambling), also contributed heavily to La Salle County's gaming reputation.

That reputation continued to flourish into the next century when in the mid-1920s, a local legend emerged. It was about this time that a stocky La Salle Irishman, Thomas J. Cawley, the son of a coal miner, quit his low-paying street car conductor job and opened a small pool hall/cigar store with Vice Kelly (who was to die before his name became famous, thanks to his partner). The business soon became well-known for the gambling that occurred there, rather than for pool or tobacco.

For the next 25 years, Cawley's notoriety as La Salle's "Czar of Gambling" grew throughout the Midwest. With the expensive blessing of local politicians and police officials, he was able to keep the Chicago mobsters from moving in on his territory. A belief evolved among many county residents (a belief that remains in the 1990s) that if vice was controlled by local men, it was a victimless activity that was acceptable to them. The affable Cawley, whose business made him wealthy and powerful, wasn't the only local who made more than a living from gambling, but he came to be the most visible one in the community.

Around 1937, foreseeing the coming world war and the public's need for diversions, he invested a bank-borrowed loan into his business for the expansion and remodeling of his tiny pool hall into an attractive, full-fledged casino. His vision was to make him a millionaire.

The legendary Kelly and Cawley's building at 641 First Street, (now known as First Street Mall), was a three-story brick structure anchored in the heart of La Salle's downtown area. On its glazed tan exterior, a huge neon sign illuminated the block in all directions. There were three front entrances, two giving access to the first floor, with the third being a doorless stairway that led up to the second floor gaming area.

The first floor had several diversions for "pocket change" gamers (mostly local residents) centered around a long bar and dining section. The popular baseball pool and football parlay betting, each in its season, attracted thousands of dollars each week, while other activities such as lucky bowls, punch boards and rows of slot machines also pulled in big money.

Instructions for all games was eagerly and politely given to any novice gamblers in the house: "Ladies and gentlemen, this game is simple. You just punch a number on the board. If you punch the lucky number, you win the prize." The prize was usually the winner's choice of items such as radios, guns, etc. which

La Salle, Illinois was known as "Little Reno" during the heyday of the illegal gaming houses in the 1930s and '40s. Famous casinos such as **Kelly and Cawley's** and **Tinny's Silver Congo** attracted thousands of people every week. On Friday and Saturday nights, hotels throughout the county were booked, the streets were lined with shops and the constant activity of both residents and eager-to-play tourists often created standing-room-only crowds on the village's sidewalks. Virtually no thought was given to the fact that most gambling was (and still is) illegal in this state.

were all prominently displayed along the back bar. The more expensive the punchboard game a customer wagered on, the better the choice of prizes would be won.

The first floor also reportedly served as an emergency "book" for horse racing bets. Results were regularly announced as the racing wire machine clattered away. Wagers from horse players were taken on the lower level during the few occasions when the "heat" temporarily forced the closing of the upper floors.

While small-time bettors won or lost downstairs, it was on the upper floors that the "heavy money" appeared. The small antigambling segments of the community charged it was on these floors that mortgage money was lost from paychecks belonging to people who couldn't afford to lose. However, Cawley and his cohorts said that well-to-do high rollers, pulled in from Chicago and other communities where gambling was more controlled, constituted the vast majority of the customers on the upper levels.

The country casino's second floor was the home of an ornate round counter bar, a huge roulette wheel, the ever-profitable book, 50-plus slot machines, poker rooms and a bandstand stage for nationally-known bands and other big name entertainers. Stars of that era such as Donald O'Connor and George Goble were contracted by Cawley to perform to standing-room-only crowds. These entertainers did much to increase the nightclub's popularity. One of the casino's former employees recalled: "One of Cawley's philosophies with the gambling was to give customers the best entertainment and keep his food and drink prices low. You could order a steak dinner for something like 50 cents or chicken for a quarter! By doing that, he attracted so many more people into the place and so made enough money from the slot machines alone to more than offset all the entertainment and food he practically gave away."

Herbie Hummer, who was the club's piano player and the house band leader for nearly 16 years, spoke of memories of the club before his death:

"Man, those were the days... everyone was having a good time! I was first hired by 'the old man' (Cawley) to play piano by myself and later on, around 1939 or '40, I put together a six-piece band for the club. We played six nights a week and the place was always busy, often to three or four o'clock in the morning. You actually had to fight the crowds on the streets and sidewalks to get from Cawley's place to the Silver Congo Club down the way.

"The entertainment was continuous in nightclubs up and down First Street. You would see the same faces night after night. Back then, there were buses running late into the night and cabs hauling people around town. The Rock Island Rocket would bring trainloads of folks down from Chicago and you couldn't find a motel or hotel room within miles of La Salle. Cawley's was a well-known place... I once saw Jack Dempsey and Dizzy Dean there!

"I often helped 'the old man' count money and, man, I'm telling you, it was like lettuce there was so much of it at times! I don't remember anyone who ever said anything bad about Tom Cawley. He had a lot of friends and treated gambling as a serious business. You had to kinda admire the guy 'cause if someone (usually a housewife) would complain that an entire paycheck was lost in the place, he would give the family the money back without much argument. The only thing that Cawley would ask was that they never come back in to play."

Commenting on the atmosphere of the period, Hummer, who played piano across the Illinois Valley until his death, said, "The attitude of the local people was better back then... The town was alive! And gambling was everywhere... They even had slot machines in the gas stations!"

As World War II ended and the nation's attention returned to domestic matters, gambling houses, which had flourished for decades across Illinois and the Midwest, began to be closed down one by one as other priorities evolved in those communities. However, Kelly and Cawley's (and many other clubs in the immediate area) continued to prosper and remain relatively untouched by authorities. Except for pre-warned sporadic raids, which only interrupted business for a mere few hours, there seemed to be no end in sight for popular gaming enterprises.

In the fall of 1947, a special grand jury impaneled by Circuit Court Judge Roy Wilhelm indicted four Illinois Valley mayors and three police chiefs on charges of malfeasance due to their failure to suppress gambling. These indictments were soon thrown out by another Circuit Judge, Frank Hayes, who termed the special grand jury "a disgrace." Judge Wilhelm termed his colleague "abusive."

"...it (the money) was like lettuce..."
Herbie Hummer

The next organized attempt at clearing out the illegal operations was initiated by the La Salle-Peru Daily News-Tribune in the fall of 1949. In front page editorials, the newspaper blasted at the conscience of the community, asserting that "legitimate business was being strangled by the flow of money to slot machines, crap tables, roulette wheels, lucky jars, horse racing and houses of prostitution."

The newspaper's demands were simple. It called for honest, efficient and competent government in La Salle County.

To maintain focus on the problem, an investigative reporter was secretly hired by the newspaper to produce a series of articles which highlighted Tom Cawley's bookie monopoly and "his total disregard for the law." The results of the News-Tribune's efforts were that several area gaming operations (not Cawley's) were closed down for a while; however, most of the houses soon reopened as the anti-gambling articles fell off the front page. Law enforcement authorities as well as the majority of the community itself were just not interested in the sincere lectures from their local newspaper. The News-Tribune burned to the ground during a huge fire in December of 1949. Although the cause was rumored to be related to the anti-gambling articles, no such connection was ever offically made public.

The start of the 1950s was the beginning of the end of the Kelly and Cawley era when Tom Cawley's path crossed that of United States Senator Estes Kefauver, an ambitious politician from Tennessee who found national prominence as he attempted to expose organized crime throughout the country. As chairman of the U. S. Senate Special Committee to Investigate Crime in Interstate Commerce, Kefauver conducted hearings across the nation that led to the already accepted conclusion that gambling in the nation was almost invariably

Thomas J. Cawley waits for another question from U. S. Senator **Estes Kefauver** during organized crime hearings held in October 1950 at the U. S. Court House in Chicago. **Cawley** shocked the investigative committee with his candor about illegal gambing operations in La Salle County.

connected with organized crime. He also publicized his contention that organized crime and political corruption went hand-in-hand in a most profitable alliance. In his personal memoirs of the congressional hearings, "**Crime in America**," Kefauver wrote:

"The pattern suggested so far (by the committee's probes) is that crime and contempt for the law are big city operations. This is not necessarily so... Had time permitted, I should have liked the Senate Crime Investigation Committee to conduct at least one complete case study of such a small-town operation. The small cities and towns, as has often been said, are the backbone of America. If corruption threatens to take over small towns, it is important that we find out about it and turn the spotlight of exposure upon it, so an aroused public opinion can get to work on cleaning up conditions.

"In many big cities, young people come to maturity with the attitude of contempt for the law, because almost daily they see and hear of instances wherein criminals, through alliances with conniving politicians and crooked law enforcement officers, are bigger that the law. It would be a frightful thing if the same disillusionment should spread to the small-town youngsters of America."

In his book, the Senator, who would later nudge aside John F. Kennedy for the 1956 vice-presidential nomination, pointed an accusing finger at La Salle. He relates the recorded testimony of the subpoenaed Cawley, who, unlike witnesses before him, surprised nearly everyone on the panel by not refusing to speak on the grounds of self-incrimination. The gambler's bold candor was publicized by the national press.

Cawley's first appearance was in executive session on October 18, 1950, at the U. S. Court House in Chicago. Associated Counsel George Robinson examining:

Q. State your full name.

A. Thomas J. Cawley.

Q. Where do you live?

A. La Salle, Illinois; born and raised there.

Q. What is your business, Mr. Cawley?

A. A cigar store operator.

Q. What other business do you have?

A. I operate a farm... and a book...

Q. Where do you operate your book?

A. 621 First Street, La Salle, Illinois.

Q. Is that the only book you operate?

A. I operate one in Streator, Illinois.

Q. Is it solely a book?

A. Well, it is a gaming room is what it is... We have dice...

Q. You also have gambling equipment?

A. Yes.

Q. What type of games do you run?

A. Dice.

Q. Crap tables?

A. That is correct.

Q. Roulette?

A. Roulette... in La Salle, and that is all.

Cawley went on to tell the hearing officials that he employed between 65 and 70 persons in his La Salle business.

Q. How long have you operated the book there?

A. I imagine... around 15 years.

Chairman Kefauver: Is that in La Salle?

A. In La Salle... at Streator, I would say 10 years.

Q. Who is the sheriff of that county?

A. The sheriff is Ryan.

Q. How long have you known him?

A. I hardly know the man...

Q. Did you know Mike Welter?

> "I operate a farm... and a book..."
> Tom Cawley

A. Yes, sir. He was sheriff three terms...

Q. Did you contribute to the campaign funds of any of the other sheriffs?

A. No, sir... only Mike Welter.

Q. How much did you contribute to his campaign?

A. Five hundred dollars.

Q. Mike Welter knew what business you were in?

A. I wouldn't know whether he would or not.

Q. Why?

A. I never asked him...

Chairman: What we want to get at is... how can you run wide open down there without the sheriff knowing about it and doing something about it? It is generally known, is it not, that you operate these places?

A. That is right. I was born and raised there. I had a good friend, the mayor of the town, and he wouldn't let none of them politicians come into our city...

Chairman: He would not let any politicians come in?

A. He wouldn't let them politicians come from the county into the city...

Chairman: He would not let the sheriff come in?

A. That is right.

Chairman: So he is the one who lets you keep on running, is that it?

A. He never let me keep on running. He didn't do any more for me than he would for anybody else. Anybody can go down in that town right today and open up... and it doesn't cost them a five-cent piece.

Chairman: The sheriff does not bother you?

A. That is right.

Chairman: Do the people like it, you think?

A. I think they do, ninety percent of them.

Q. What is the present chief of police's name?

A. Eddie Kasprowicz, something like that...

Q. He knows what business you're in?

A. Yes. Everybody in town knows what business I am in.

Q. Do you pay money for protection?

A. No, sir.

Q. Never had paid any money?

A. No. When I do, I will get out of business.

Q. Do you contribute any money to political parties?

A. I might contribute to both parties a check, a hundred here or a hundred there... yes.

Q. Have the mayor or chief of police ever done anything to put down your book?

A. No.

Further questioning revealed more of Cawley's business connections, including the racing wire service he used. The astounded officials pressed Cawley for more details, but the shrewd businessman sidestepped their questions easily. Following his return from Chicago, La Salle city officials, embarrassed by the national publicity, publicly ordered that Kelly and Cawley's be shut down. However, a different story unfolded when Cawley was summoned again before the committee on Dec. 20 with Robinson again leading the questions:

Q. Do you still have an establishment in both places?

A. That is correct.

Q. Are they still operating?

A. That is right.

Q. Have they been down to speak of for any period of time in the last two or three months?

A. Very little.

Q. You have no trouble operating now?

A. That is right.

Q. Everything is going the same as usual?

A. Yes.

Q. Your books are operating... and your crap tables are operating?

A. That is correct.

The candid witness went on to enumerate, in response to the committee's inquires, details of the various games that he controlled at his clubs. He told them about the horse books, the punchboards, the poker games, the sports pools and the roulette wheels. The amazed Kefauver picked up the questioning:

Q. How do you account for the fact that you can operate the way you can, Mr. Cawley?

A. Well, it has been going on down there for 25 years...

Q. You said 90 percent of the people like it?

A. That is right. We had an election down there that proved that.

Q. Tell me about that...

A. The sheriff... two sheriffs run... one run on an anti-gambling ticket and the other fellow run on an open ticket, and the fellow on the open ticket won the election...

Q. Don't you sell liquor in your places?

A. ... they took my liquor license away from me.

Q. And when did they take the liquor license away from you?

A. After I got back from this meeting the last time (laughter from the observers echoed through the hearing room).

Q. But you still sell liquor?

A. That is right,

Q. But it hasn't made any difference in your operation?

A. No.

Despite increased pressure on county and city officials to close down the now-even more famous gaming house following the Senate hearings, Cawley again beat the odds. Business went on and went on well. Well, that is, until a young lawyer named Harland D. Warren was elected La Salle County State's Attorney in the fall of 1952.

Born into a farming family whose ancestors were among the first pioneers to settle in the county, Harland Warren grew up on a 150-acre homestead in Serena Township, 13 miles north of Ottawa. He attended local schools and majored in business and political science before graduating from law school at the University of Illinois. He maintained his interest in law and government during the four years he served in World War II on board amphibious units in the U. S. Navy Reserve.

Warren, an intensely honest man, returned home from the war to find gambling, prostitution and liquor interests virtually controlling law enforcement agencies from one end of the county to the other. Fed up with the corruption and encouraged by many friends, the attorney won the Republican nomination for the county prosecutor's job early in 1952. He then began a vigorous campaign, barnstorming every town to promise that he would rid the county of all vice and remain immune from any tempting monetary influences.

The electorate acknowledged their disgust with the gambling problem by electing the crusading Warren that fall. Minutes after he was sworn into office, the new state's attorney made it clear to all city mayors and police agencies that the era of widespread corruption was over. "Gambling and prostitution cannot exist in a city if the police chief wants to do his job!" he insisted in post-election interviews.

A short time later, a stone shattered a front window at his home, an apparent warning to keep hands off the local rackets.

Unafraid, Warren began to crack down on illegal bingo games at local churches, cash-paying pinball machines, local lotteries and even removed the several slot machines at his own Elk's Club (an act to which fellow members never forgave him). Warren also decided to strike boldly at the heart of the county's most flagrant gambling center by initiating an investigation of Kelly and Cawley's.

Using his own personal money, the new state's attorney hired two private detectives from Chicago to assemble detailed evidence against the La Salle business, "because I couldn't trust any of the local officials." The investigation, for which the county later reimbursed Warren, didn't take long.

The handwriting on the wall marking the end of Cawley's reign occurred as Warren, flanked by county deputies, personally led a raid on the "cigar store" during the afternoon of Feb. 21, 1953. That particular date was chosen deliberately to further aggravate his adversary Cawley, Warren later admitted as the reasoning became apparent.

Booty from the raid included two crap tables, a roulette table, poker tables, cards, chips, a bingo barrel and such racing paraphernalia as scratch sheets, racing newspapers, form sheets and cards. Without the customary warning, Cawley's crew didn't even have a chance to switch the new working gaming tables with the worn ones stored away.

Even as Warren and his deputies listed the items to be confiscated, telephones in a cashier's cage on the second floor rang constantly. Smiling, the prosecutor answered some of the calls himself, telling Cawley's customers that there would no bets taken today. Utilizing a state commerce commission regulation that prohibited use of telephones for illegal operations, Warren later contacted the phone company, which soon removed the equipment.

The raiders had no warrants for the arrest of any particular individuals, since it was not known who would be present on the property that Saturday. Instead, Warren politely requested that Cawley and the few employees in the building come to the county courthouse in Ottawa to have formal charges preferred against them there. Amazingly, the gamblers agreed without protest.

The reason for Warren's weekend timing of the raid soon became obvious as Cawley stood before a

Kelly & Cawley's was the centerpoint of **La Salle's** legendary gambling era. It was located in the heart of the downtown business section. The small casino attracted players, both amateur and professional, from all over the country.

judge to arrange bond for himself and his workers. The state's attorney strongly insisted that only cash bonds be posted to the court in order for the accused men to obtain release. The judge agreed and declined to accept Cawley's or anyone else's personal check.

It was a Saturday. The banks were closed. And Monday (as Warren knew only too well) was Washington's birthday. No local bank would be open for three days.

Those present that day in the courtroom said later it was the first time they had ever seen Tom Cawley angry. "I've been in things before," he snapped at reporters swarming the courthouse hallways, "and I've always been able to sign my own bond before! If he (Warren) doesn't think I'm worth the money, he can check my Dunn and Bradstreet rating!"

Warren was out to signal every La Salle County resident that breaking the law in his jurisdiction would no longer be tolerated and the penalty would no longer be a slap on the wrist. He had purposely made it difficult for Cawley to come up with that much cash for bail in the hope that a few hours behind bars in the county jail would prove to the "czar" that it would never be business as usual during his term in office.

Scrambling for the cash, the visibly-shaken Cawley quickly called some Ottawa business associates. Soon that evening, after a nearby bank was quietly opened and the bonds were paid, he and his men were released.

Warren had shown Cawley that he was not bluffing about putting an end to La Salle's

The raid on **Kelly & Cawley's** in 1952 signaled the end of the wide-open gambling period of La Salle County. Truckloads of illegal gaming equipment and other paraphernalia were hauled out of the popular establishment. During the next few years, one-by-one, the famous gaming saloons closed or were shut down.

national reputation as a "wide-open-town." The cigar store owner was later fined several thousand dollars for operating a gambling house. During the short trial, Cawley's popularity with local officials was illustrated by a high-ranking policemen who testified with a straight face that he had been in the accused's cigar store several times and swore under oath that he had never seen any gambling take place.

Soon after his conviction, Cawley grew weary of continued investigations by county officials. Fearing that another arrest could result in a jail sentence, the smart businessman decided to take the money and run. He poured his fortune into a real estate business, where he again was successful.

The old man's nephew, Ryan Cawley, remembering the famous club, said, "When I first started with Tom as a kid, I had no idea that what we were doing was illegal. We also thought that it would last forever..." Thomas J. Cawley died on January 18, 1961.

Other small-time bookmakers and vice leaders in the county "saw the handwriting on the wall" and gradually closed up their open gambling establishments with Warren's strong encouragement. The names of popular hangouts such as Club 359, Tinney's Silver Congo, El Mirador, The Stables, The Rocket Inn, Denny's Tavern, The Twin Bars, The Senate, The Empire, Little Jimmy's Club 109, The Gay Mill, The Cotton Club, The Rose Bowl and Kelley and Cawley's are now only memories.

The fever continues, however. Gambling in La Salle County is not entirely just a memory. Despite more police raids on various local taverns and clubs during the late 1950s and '60s which resulted in regular arrests and confiscation of enough gaming devices to fill a building, they did little to discourage local residents from gambling. Locals, many of whom had been raised on tip boards and sports parlays, continue to take a chance on various gaming options at their favorite tavern or restaurant.

The 1970s produced less spectacular raids which were just as ineffective in eradicating the inbred gambling habits of La Salle County citizens. However, by standards set in the Kelly and Cawley era, the games were at least restricted to far less flagrant operations.

In the 1990s, the "victimless crime" continues throughout the county in neighborhood pubs, at social functions, even at community and church bazaars. Tip boards and other gambling paraphernalia continue to be seized by county and state police authorities in sporadic raids of various area businesses. Faced with simple fines, the owners of these establishments often reopen their doors a mere few hours after being "closed down." As the long-dead Tom Cawley noted decades before: occasional court fines were simply the cost of doing business.

An analysis of La Salle County gambling history would not be complete without comment on the Illinois State Lottery and the state's recent excursion into riverboat gambling operations. Taking the attitude of "if you can't beat 'em, join 'em," state legislators legalized their own form of controlled gambling with the creation of the state lottery in 1974. The rationale was that the lottery would raise millions of dollars to fund state schools and other projects without the imposition of additional taxes. In fact, many state officials refer to the lottery as a "voluntary tax." However, despite the state's publicized good intentions, a moral question has been voiced constantly and consistently through the past many years: should citizens be encouraged to participate in games of chance that rob them of their basic resources with little hope of any substantial return? Legislators who supported the state lottery's creation claim that legalized betting takes gambling dollars out of the hands of organized crime. But those who oppose the games contend that rather than making gambling honest, lottery legalization only makes the government corrupt.

Former Maryland Governor Harry Hughes said, "Legalized gambling is not a good way to finance special (state) projects because it takes money away from those who can least afford it." On the other side, David Ellis of the Massachusetts Lottery Commission has been quoted as saying, "I think people understand that they benefit (from lotteries) even if they don't play. It is a form of voluntary tax and everybody (here) is pretty comfortable with it."

What can't be argued is the fact that both the Illinois State Lottery and the state's riverboat casinos are both overwhelming successes. Illinois Gaming Board and state lottery officials have reported that the state-controlled games have generated billions of dollars since their creation, making the lottery one of the largest revenue producers in the state. Legislators also point to the success of riverboat gambling throughout the state as a reason to continue studies of additional gaming options to help fund the state's future.

Despite that undeniable success, former Illinois Governor Jim Thompson once cautioned groups of state business leaders that the state should not become too dependent on the lottery income because, "there's no guarantee it will continue to be a success." Thompson said that the money should not be used for everyday operations, but instead should be held to fund what he called "extras," or "things that are nice to do when you have the money but can be put off if you don't in any particular year."

According to recent Associated Press reports, all but a handful of states now have some form of legalized gambling, from Alaska where residents wager on when the ice will break up in the China and Tanana rivers every spring, to Florida where citizens bet millions daily on horse, dogs and *jai alai* games.

The reports stated that Americans place more than $50 billion in legal games and possibly several times that number in illegal activities each year. That staggering amount averages well over $200 for every adult and child in the country. Opponents to all forms of gambling point to those figures as one way out of the national deficit that continues to blacken America's future.

As for gambling being a "way of life" here in the Illinois Valley, that notion was pretty well confirmed with a series of raids conducted by state and federal agencies on April 9, 1996. Dubbed "Operation Tip-Off," law enforcement officials swooped into 30 area taverns and restaurants, arresting nearly 25 people and confiscating truckloads of gaming paraphernalia. Not surprisingly, reaction from local residents was not mixed. The vast majority of those interviewed by local media defended the business owners against the intrusion of government, laughing at the reports that the agencies have been working two years verifying the evidence for the raids. One area resident joked, "I could have done it in two hours!" Gambling on pull tabs and tip boards is simply considered a way of life in La Salle County. Most of the establishments raided that day were open for business that very night or the next day. Business as usual...

The debate rages as the fever continues.

This aerial view of the summit of the Rock at **Starved Rock State Park** near **Utica** shows the intricate wooden platforms which now encircle the tourist attraction. The decking was built by the state in 1981 to help prevent erosion caused by the hundreds of thousands of visitors each year.

MASSACRE AT INDIAN CREEK

The year was 1832.

For 15 weeks that summer, the once-peaceful Illinois Valley became a fearful place to live for both native American Indian tribes and migratory white pioneers. Senseless abuses of century-old Indian encampments by the new settlers resulted in a bloody short war throughout Central Illinois which produced little but suffering for both sides.

It became known as the Black Hawk War.

The pivotal point in the hostilities came during a warm afternoon on May 20 along the banks of Indian Creek, near what is now Shabbona Park, north of Ottawa. In the sad history of Indian/pioneer conflicts, that tragic event remains a relatively small footnote in the nation's heritage. However, the actions of a few frustrated and enraged warriors on that balmy day became the catalyst that ultimately drove thousands of Illinois-born Indians forever westward across the Mississippi River.

The respected Indian leader, Black Sparrow Hawk, a self-proclaimed chief from the Saukenuk village (composed of both Sauk and Fox tribesmen) near the Rock River, began his short-lived uprising against the whites in the spring of 1832. Black Hawk and his people angrily resented the intruders on their land due to years of confrontations. Treaties forced upon the many tribes by evil whites had been broken on a regular basis. The red man saw the settlers not as the heroic pioneers depicted in history books, but rather as liars and cheats who took everything and yielded nothing.

> "The more I see of the militia, the less confidence I have of their effecting anything of importance."
>
> Colonel Zachary Taylor

Black Hawk's fame among his people grew as he took up arms against the invading whites and other Indian enemies during the first few decades of the 1800s. He was revered as a mighty warrior whose tomahawk could unite the scattered and unorganized tribes throughout the Midwest.

Interracial discontent began its escalation into war during the winter of 1828 when Black Hawk's beloved home village, left vacant as was customary in the cold hunting season, was overrun by white settlers. The proud chief's own lodge was invaded by these trespassers who refused to leave upon the return of the tribe. Other lodges within the camp were found destroyed or severely damaged.

History records that Black Hawk first attempted to evict the invaders by peaceful means, seeking justice from both state and federal governments. Illinois Governor Ninian Edwards and Superintendent of U. S. Indian Affairs Gen. William Clark, pointing to a deceptive treaty signed by unauthorized chiefs, ignored Black Hawk's plea for justice, ordering instead that the village and the land around it to be sold to the settlers.

The decision infuriated the Indians, who believed that the land could not be bought or sold because it existed as a basic right for those who cultivated and hunted on it. Ironically, that was essentially the same rationalization the whites used to force the land from the natives.

Other chieftains, aware that armed resistance against the white power was doomed to certain failure, avoided sure bloodshed by moving their tribes across the Mississippi into Iowa.

Black Hawk refused. He told his departing fellow tribe members that he would make war against the entire white nation— alone, if necessary. However, despite his intense anger, the warrior and his militant followers were finally persuaded by well-meaning government officials to leave Illinois peacefully. Before crossing the mighty river, Black Hawk told the Army authorities that he would try to live his life without war.

Black Hawk's peaceful retirement ended in the middle of 1831 as government agents again reneged on treaty agreements and committed further atrocities against his people. Despite overtures from many peace seekers within his tribes, the leader began his echoing war chant during the winter of 1831, vowing to recapture his homeland from the whites the following spring. The chief used the cold months to send young runners to various Indian factions throughout the Midwest to recruit young braves for his war party.

Other Indian leaders, including Shabbona, chief of a small band of Pottawatomi tribes, once again campaigned throughout northern Illinois to resist the temptations to start a war that could not be won. They conceded that Black Hawk was indeed a brave warrior but said he was misguided by false Indian prophets. The chiefs insisted there would never be an end to the white nuisance.

The Great Indian Leader Black Hawk

65

Black Hawk returned to his beloved Illinois prairie in early 1832 with only one-sixth of his displaced tribe, which included women, children and old men. Crossing the Mississippi near the mouth of the Iowa River, the determined group headed north, expecting to be met by large numbers of sympathetic warriors along the way. Before the month was over, however, it was apparent to the Indian leader that, beyond a few hot-headed braves, no serious support for his cause was to come from other tribes. The number of actual fighting men never numbered over 200 souls.

Feeling betrayed, Black Hawk considered retracing his tracks back into Iowa, but he soon felt encouraged by reports that his wary party had spread panic among the area's settlers. Organized by U. S, military officials, many of these homesteaders joined the militia on a temporary basis to battle the Indian threat. Among the more than 1,500 volunteers were future U. S. Presidents Abraham Lincoln (who never participated in any real fighting) and Colonel Zachary Taylor. Together with regular Army troops, the motley militia began to follow Black Hawk's trail, forcing the Indians forward along the Rock River.

The first of the supposedly formidable army force neared the small renegade war party 30 miles north of Dixon's Ferry, a tiny settlement operated by John Dixon. Led by Major Isaiah Stillman, the 275 volunteers, untrained and undisciplined, unwittingly had made camp on May 15 only a few miles from the group they were chasing over the prairie.

Informed by alert scouts of the troop's close proximity, Black Hawk sent messengers back to Dixon's Ferry with a white flag of truce to avoid bloodshed and open peace negotiations. The sight of brown warriors entering their camp, regardless of their white flag and friendly intentions, so frightened the nervous volunteers that many of them began shooting at them. Several of the emissaries were killed. The survivors raced back to their camp with the troops in hot pursuit.

Learning that his offer of peace had been scorned, an enraged Black Hawk hurriedly gathered fewer than 50 braves for what he considered a suicide stand against the advancing whites. The chief later said that he expected this to be his last battle, as his warriors were so outnumbered. As the militia riders broke into the clearing the braves startled the troops with a flurry of arrows, gunshots and war cries. Despite the odds against them, the Indians terrified the attackers into an awkward and hasty retreat.

The soldiers and volunteers scattered into the night in all directions, some not stopping until they had reached the safety of their own homesteads 40 or 50 miles away. A premature report on the incident to government officials listed more than 50 whites "slaughtered" in the fierce battle that came to be known as Stillman's Run. The actual number missing was only 11 men.

The humiliating defeat of Stillman's Run quickly swelled into legend throughout the forested frontier. The exaggerated story alarmed Illinois settlers, many of whom quickly proceeded to take their families to the safe shelter of established forts. Additional settlers enlisted into the ranks of the militia force, but Colonel Taylor of the U.S. Regulars was quoted as saying, "The more I see of the militia, the less confidence I have of their effecting anything of importance." The greatly falsified reports of massive Indian strength also inspired formerly peaceful braves to take up arms against their white neighbors. It was this fanciful sense of possible victory over the oppressive pioneers that was to doom 15 innocent people along Indian Creek and eventually transplant whole nations of guiltless Indians.

Once there were 40,000 square miles of prairie surrounding the Starved Rock area.

William Davis was a storybook stereotype of a homesteader. He was a brawny man blessed with hard muscles developed over many years of pounding red-hot metal as a Kentucky blacksmith. In 1830, Davis moved north with his wife and eight children to carve a life out of the Illinois dirt. They settled on the bank of Indian Creek, 12 miles north of Ottawa, where Davis handcrafted a cabin and blacksmith shack.

Life in La Salle County was good for the hardworking Davis family. They raised livestock in their green meadow and yellow corn in their fields. With Ottawa and the military fort only 12 miles to the south, they felt a sense of security from any possible Indian uprisings. Several native villages, including Chief Shabbona's camp, were close to them, each feeding off the clear waters of the small creek. For the most part, the tribes came to accept if not ignore their white neighbors.

The beauty and natural resources of the Indian Creek settlement soon attracted others: the John Hendersons, the William Pettigrews and their two children, the William Halls and their six children, and the

Shabbona

Albert Howards. The small colony was growing cabin by cabin, and the homesteaders began to nourish a dream. They imagined that a populated village was to grow around them (actually the number of whites in the entire county was less than 150 permanent residents).

As the spring of 1832 approached, Davis and his neighbors began work on a grist mill in order to process their own grain, eliminating a regular wagon trip to Ottawa. The first step in the project was to build a dam on the creek. They worked swiftly, but as the project neared completion, Davis and his men often awoke to find the dirt and stone dam damaged, apparently by Indians who resented the intrusion their vital fishing streams.

Early one May day, Davis caught two young Indians destroying the dam. The homesteader, enraged and swinging a large hickory stick, severely beat the culprits as a warning to them and other braves to stay clear of the settlement. As they limped away, the humiliated natives swore revenge. Davis shrugged off the threat. He would never fear two young bucks.

A few days later, while Davis was away from the settlement, a familiar Indian figure rode a sweating pony into his clearing. The tired rider, Chief Shabbona, had learned of impending attacks on whites by frustrated

Indians encouraged by the "victory" at Stillman's Run. In sign language and broken English, the heavy-set red man begged his neighbors to journey south to ensure safety. The concerned chief then remounted his horse (which was destined to collapse dead from exhaustion before his ride was over) to spread the alarm to other white settlements in the surrounding area. After little discussion, the Indian Creek settlers quickly collected themselves and headed south.

Davis, returning home, was surprised to meet the caravan of his family and friends on the prairie. Hearing their story, he reminded them that they had once before needlessly fled their homes following similar warnings in the spring of the previous year. He also remembered his self-imposed promise that he would never be run off his own land again. The group was persuaded to return with the leader to the settlement.

Although they chose to ignore Shabbona's plea, the pioneers did decide there was safety in numbers and, for the sake of the women and children within the group, they stayed together in the Davis cabin. Unafraid of any invisible threat and encouraged by the fresh spring weather, the settlers eventually returned to their daily chores in the days that followed the warning.

On May 20, 1832, the settlement's newly-cleared field was wet. Soaked from weeks of heavy thunderstorms, the black earth stuck to the boots of the prairie farmers as they painstakingly planted the corn one kernel at a time in monotonous motions. The warm sun pulled moisture up from the dirt into their faces, soaking the settlers in their own sweat.

Several other men and youngsters spent most of that day wading and working around the settlement's dam. Large stones were rolled and smaller ones carried in an effort to repair the damage done earlier by the young Indians. Vital to the encampment's survival, the dam pushed the creek water back upon its banks. Water power from the stone barrier would provide power to grind the fall harvest and add hope to the dream of a permanent village.

As the sun fell, the women and children were huddled together some 50 feet from the creek's north bank. The younger girls sewed blankets, while the mothers worked on the evening meal.

On the settlement's outskirts, unknown to the busy squatters, a band of renegade Indians silently watched them. Their number was later estimated to be between 40 and 70 braves, mostly from the Potowatomi tribe, along with some of Black Hawk's warriors. Hidden in the thick foliage lining the creek, the painted natives waited for the right moment to begin the assault. They would attack from the west, shielded for a moment by the setting sun.

About half past four o'clock, some of the men gathered in the crude blacksmith shop to share a drink from a bucket of water. Looking out into the field on the creek's south side, the resting men could easily see their friends sowing corn. They spoke about the coming summer, the fall harvest and the future expansion of their settlement.

The attack on the **Indian Creek** settlers was the catalyst which eventually forced most of the midwest native American tribes westward across the Mississippi River.

Suddenly, the barking of Davis' dog and a single scream of terror pierced the afternoon quiet. Another voice shouted, "There are the Indians now!"

The bushes and prairie grass to the west of the clearing yielded wave after wave of shrieking warriors until the encampment was surrounded. Those few Indians with guns fired at the startled whites. Bullets ripped through the smithy shed as the settlers dove out of the way. Screaming at the top of their lungs, the Indians swooped down upon the outnumbered pioneers.

Reacting quickly, Davis and

his companions grabbed rifles and hand tools for protection. The leader himself held an unloaded rifle at face level and led a charge toward the attackers.

William Pettigrew was near the main cabin's doorway as warriors advanced toward it. He attempted to shut and block the door but was immediately overpowered. A shot thundered in his ears and a bullet tore through Pettigrew's chest, his blood splattering across the unfinished blankets. Tomahawks slammed into his head and ended his life.

Mrs. Pettigrew, her baby son in her arms, reached out to shield 15-year-old Rachel Hall. As she did, a brave stuck a rifle point blank to her face and fired. Rachel, deafened by the blast, felt the sting of burning gunpowder on her eyes and forehead. The baby fell from his dead mother's hands onto the dirt floor. The wailing child was swooped up by a warrior, who quickly raced out of the cabin into the yard. Screeching insanely, his face a mass of painted, throbbing veins, the Indian jerked the infant upside down, holding him by his heels. He moved toward a small tree trunk.

The attack became a series of brief flashes to William Hall's son, John, who stood near the black-smith shed. The cries of the Pettigrew baby forced his attention away from his father and the others just as they collided with the first wave of assailants. John turned toward the cabin to see a red man swing the inverted baby. The image of the baby's head striking the jagged stump froze in his mind as did the sound of the thud. The warrior hooted his victory over the dead child to the sky.

John looked back at his father. William Hall was now on the ground, the shirt over his left breast was stained red. The hairless arms of three Indians, each clutching crude weapons made of stone tied to wood, reached for the wounded man. John heard his father choke out, "Dear God..." An instant later, the pioneer was dead. The son took a short step toward his slain father, but upon looking across the clearing, saw even more braves enter the yard.

The father of the small colony, William Davis, stood 20 yards from the boy, the empty rifle still in his hands. With the stock now splintered, he continued to swing it at the Indians who surrounded him. He fell under the crushing blows of flying hatchets.

The young Hall boy, sobbing as he ran, fled toward the creek. The screaming braves followed in wild pursuit. In the distance, he could see more Indians on horseback, apparently placed there to prevent anyone's escape. In his blind panic, he ran off the creek's 12-foot embankment. Rolling, he came up on his feet, stunned but unhurt. The attackers knelt at the top of the embankment and raised their rifles. Ahead of John by several yards, Robert Norris and Henry George also scrambled down the creekbed. They had eluded harm from the assault in the yard and were fleeing to the south. Shots rang out. Instinctively, John dropped his head as he heard the gunballs whiz past his ears. The two runners in front of him groaned softly and dropped like stones into the water. Shot in the back, Norris stretched out a hand for help as John jumped over him. Too terrified to stop, the boy continued along the rocky creek, stumbling as he pumped his legs. Moments later, he heard the cries of his friends as they were brutally murdered. Then the only sound he heard was of his own hard breathing and the crunch of the brush under his running feet. He ran and ran and never looked back.

In the settlement's yard, the horror of the surprise attack was not over, even though most of the settlers were now dead or dying. To celebrate the ultimate victory over their slain enemies, sharp knives were drawn and pushed into the dead men's chests. Red, wet hearts, held high by dark hands, signaled the end of the attack. As was tradition, many braves tore huge bites out the fresh muscles in defiant conquest. Singing and screaming, other bodies were similarly mutilated.

Following the gun blast that burned her face and killed Mrs. Pettigrew, Rachel Hall had fallen back onto her sister, Sylvia. The two sisters pulled the bloodstained blankets over their heads as if the thin cloth would hide them from harm. Beneath the quilt, they shivered as they heard their family and friends being butchered. They screamed as the blanket was suddenly yanked off to reveal the cabin filled with painted warriors and dead bodies.

Fully expecting the same fate, they were instead pulled to their feet by several braves and half-carried out to the yard. The girls, each held tight by two Indians, were dragged into the nearby woods and then thrown up on ponies. The sun was nearly gone as the other warriors returned from their attack. Even though the sisters did not understand the captor's language, they did sense that there was an argument about whether or not they should be killed on the spot.

To take one or two prisoners in a raid as a symbol of superiority over their enemies was not uncommon for Indians of that time. Often these captives were adopted by the family of a deceased warrior and eased into the tribe. In any case, hostages were generally treated with humanity and surprising kindness.

Led by braves on foot, the horses carrying the Hall girls and the war party traveled north for several days. The group rested occasionally to eat scaled beans and roasted red oak acorns. The frightened girls

Artist's conception of the abduction of **Rachel and Sylvia Hall**.

did not utter a single word while the band rode forward through the grasslands.

Some time later, they arrived at a Sauk Camp in present day Wisconsin, some 90 miles north of the Indian Creek battleground. The captives were welcomed by several squaws, who fed them parched Indian corn meal with maple sugar. That first night in the camp, the victorious warriors again celebrated with dances and feasting for long hours.

Packing up the next day, the braves and their prisoners continued north. Before sunset, the party rode into a much larger Indian encampment and, upon seeing the white girls, the entire camp broke into a frenzy of excitement. The capture of the Hall sisters was thought to be the first of many coming victories over the white man. That night, the girls' faces were painted half black and half red. They were then led to a clearing where tribesmen had erected a ring of spears around a tall pole. There, the girls were subjected to a victory celebration that included being forced to parade around the bloody scalps which belonged to their parents and friends.

Slowly, over the next few days, Rachel and Sylvia Hall began to lose their fear of being killed. At one point during the ordeal, after a brave had tossed away Rachel's haircomb, she defiantly snatched it back. The sisters also would not allow their captors to take their shoes in exchange for moccasins.

On the fifth day following their arrival in the main camp, the girls were suddenly handed over to Winnebago tribesmen. The leader, Chief White Crow, told them that they were to be ransomed back to the white man. Although encouraged by the hope of release, the girls did not believe him.

In the meantime, the alarm that settlers felt after the Stillman Run episode turned to panic and rage as word spread of the murders at Indian Creek. The young John Hall had led a company of citizens and troops from Ottawa to the scene of the carnage. Within the clearing, they buried the mutilated dead and quickly organized for pursuit of the war party, which was known to have kidnapped the Hall girls. Picking up additional volunteers along the way, the whites gave chase northward.

While the troops advanced, negotiations for the sisters began between White Crow and Henry Gratiot, a U. S. government Indian agent. Ransom was eventually set at $2,000 worth of ponies. The elated girls were soon released near White Oak Springs, Wisconsin, following the delivery of the horses.

Days later, while returning south with their saviors, the girls were surprised to be reunited with their brother, John, whom they thought had surely been slain in the attack.

Rachel and Sylvia slowly recovered from their ordeal and later married to begin new homesteads within La Salle and Morgan counties.

The Illinois Valley Indian tribes were not so fortunate. The prejudice against them, blatant before the Indian Creek incident, was now fueled into fury against all Illinois nations. Under great pressure from citizens, state and federal government officials demanded a halt to any further hostilities against white settlements.

Their solution? Kill or displace all Indians from the Illinois plain.

The next few years found ancient Illinois Indian tribes besieged by government troops and forced to flee to the west. The white invasion, which was bent on destroying all cultural patterns of the natives, rapidly continued at the cost of human dignity. The new "civilization" that took root in the Midwest would no longer tolerate any deadly rebellion such as the Black Hawk War. The few Indians allowed to remain in Illinois represented only a handful who occupied the region.

As for the rebels themselves, Black Hawk and his men were tracked and hunted until the leader was captured and imprisoned in August 1832. The spirit of any possible resurgence of Indian dignity through warfare died with his apprehension.

> "Our young men are as numerous as the leaves in the woods."
> President Andrew Jackson

Black Hawk, an object of the white man's curiosity, was not left to waste in prison, but instead, the defeated warrior was forced on a tour of the Eastern seaboard. The trip included a personal audience with U. S. President Andrew Jackson, who told the chief, "Our young men are as numerous as the leaves in the woods."

The wrinkled Indian, astounded by the white man's vast technology, finally came to grudgingly accept that his fellow Indian leaders who had warned him not to battle the whites were correct. Black Hawk was eventually released and returned to live out his life in a remote Iowa Indian village. However, even in death, the legendary warrior was not allowed to rest. His body was stolen, as the skeleton of famous Indian leaders was a status symbol for certain whites in those times. After much protesting and threats by his kinsmen, the corpse was ultimately reinterred.

The one La Salle County Indian who escaped the repercussions stemming from the Indian Creek attack was Shabbona. Although he was hailed as a hero by local whites, the red man found himself branded a traitor by his own race because he had warned settlers of impending attacks. The homesteaders gave land to Shabbona and never forgot the honor that he had sacrificed to save human lives.

Crude cabins, such as this restored log home at **Goose Lake Prairie Preserve** south of Morris, Illinois, were carved out of the Illinois prairie as bold pioneers built homesteads.

On October 9, 1834, three Potawatomi tribe members were brought into La Salle County Circuit Court on murder charges stemming from the Indian Creek attack. The braves were soon discharged from all further liability after Mrs. Rachel (Hall) Munson, who had married shortly after her release, failed to identify any of them at the trial.

The sad and inevitable clash of the two vastly diverse societies continued throughout the rest of the century and, in many ways, remains with the nation today. History reveals that the problem was much more complex than simply what was right and what was wrong. In no way could anyone expect such a radical change to take place without betrayals, tragedies and bloodshed. Of course, both sides had their villains and their heroes.

The ill-fated Indian Creek pioneers were individually innocent of any really serious crime against the Illinois American Native nation. They merely represented a disease, a cancer that the natives thought needed to be purged from their land. True, their story is just a footnote in American history; nevertheless, their memories and deaths live on as classic examples of human misunderstandings and failings.

The bloodstained vest of **William Hall** and the bullet-riddled bonnet of his wife are some of many exhibits to be found at the La Salle County Historical Society Museum in **Utica**. The museum, located in a restored I-M Canal building, houses thousands of artifacts from the county's rich heritage and is open to the public each week. The center is also accessible to students during the school year.

The now demolished **St. Mary's Hospital** served the Illinois Valley Community for nearly 90 years. The health care center, founded by three sisters of the Francescan Order of the Sacred Heart in 1887, was located on Baker Avenue in **La Salle**. In 1975 St. Mary's Hospital was ordered by the Illinois Department of Public Health to replace several buildings within two years to meet state fire protection and design codes. It was soon determined that it would not be economically feasible to construct new facilities for a variety of reasons. Later that same year, St. Mary's merged with the more modern **People's Hospital** in Peru forming a new health corporation: **Illinois Valley Community Hospital**. The aging facility was soon permanently closed and has been transformed into the **Illinois Veteran's Home at La Salle**.

THE STARVED ROCK MURDERS

The year was 1960.

On Monday, March 14, Mildred Lindquist, 50; Lillian Oetting, 50; and Frances Murphy, 47, drove from their expensive neighborhood homes in Riverside, Illinois to historic Starved Rock State Park outside Ottawa for a four-day holiday. Mrs. Oetting, who had spent most of that winter nursing her ill husband following a heart attack, talked quietly with her two companions during the 92-mile drive about the upcoming few days of hiking and bird-watching.

Employees of the park's lodge would later recall the women's arrival. Frances Murphy parked her gray Ford station wagon in the inn's parking area and the friends unloaded their few pieces of luggage. They registered for two rooms, took their bags there and ate a quick lunch in the rustic dining room.

Around 1:15 p.m., lodge caretaker Emil Boehm noticed the women leave the lobby. One of the ladies turned to him and said, "It's a beautiful day for a hike."

"Yes, ma'am," Boehm replied, barely looking up from his work.

Over Mrs. Oetting's shoulder hung a 35mm Argus C-3 camera in a brown leather case complete with strap. Mrs. Murphy, who actually owned the camera, carried a small pair of binoculars.

St. Louis Canyon-the most breathtaking and unlikely scene of the crime.

The women, who all attended the Riverside Presbyterian Church, walked in rubber galoshes through light, slippery snow along a narrow trail, taking photographs of each other on the way. Eventually, they came to the dead end of St. Louis Canyon, whose rocky walls rise 80 feet on three sides framing a majestic frozen waterfall. The women were only a mile from the lodge.

Photographing the scene, the three close friends then turned to leave and hiked into a horror that stunned the Illinois Valley and the nation — a horror that would ultimately consume thousands of detective man-hours and affect law enforcement agencies across the state.

According to Indian lore, a war party from the Fox tribe surrounded a small number of their bitter enemies, the Illinois, on a huge rock overlooking the Illinois River in 1769. Legend has it that the Illinois warriors were besieged on the rock, starved into submission and then, brutally slaughtered.

Centuries later, that Indian battleground is now the 2,022-acre state park known as Starved Rock, a recreational haven for visitors from all over the world. For decades, the park was a place of picnics and peace.

Then, in March 1960, the legend of past violence became a harsh reality with the discovery of the bludgeoned bodies of the three socially-prominent women. Found in one of the park's altar-like box canyons, the murders threw the entire Illinois Valley into a panic.

Christened from violence, Starved Rock had lived up to its name.

Few know that the story of the Starved Rock murders actually began on September 13, 1959 as a young couple strolled through the quiet woods of Matthiessen State Park, located less than a mile south of Starved Rock. The girl, happy in her final year of high school, had taken time away from studies for a short walk with her older boyfriend.

The couple hiked along the long trails of Matthiessen until they reached the Little Vermilion River, a natural boundary at the back end of the park. Suddenly, a man materialized out of the forest. He carried a single shot rifle in his hand. Even as the armed man approached, the boy and girl thought little about it.

"What time is it?" the stranger asked.

"6:30...," the boy answered.

The man turned back up the trail. The couple, noticing that daylight was rapidly fading, headed toward their car.

Without warning, the man appeared behind them. "Turn around," he said. "I've got this rifle pointed at you." They looked back to see the stranger, his gun and the bullet held between his teeth.

Motioning with the rifle, the man forced the couple toward the river again and, without protest, they obeyed. Once there, he tied the boy with thin fishing line, gagged him and took his wallet. The assailant faced the girl. Taking her a few feet away from the boy, he slowly ripped her clothes away with a knife. Terrified, she begged him to stop. The boyfriend, helpless, closed his eyes, listening to the sounds of the rape. A few minutes later, the attacker tied the girl with pieces of her own clothing. He told them in quiet tones that he would return if he heard any screams for help. Turning, he disappeared into the timber with the last light of day.

The shaken couple quickly broke free of their bonds and ran arm-in-arm through the dark forest to the parking lot. Following a short trip to the girl's house (her parents were not home), they drove to the La Salle County Sheriff's Department in Ottawa. There the sobbing girl was escorted by deputies to the local hospital where she underwent a thorough examination. She was

State and county police investigators sift through freshly fallen snow in **St. Louis Canyon** to uncover vital clues to the Illinois Valley area's most shocking mass murder mystery.

questioned in the emergency room about the incident, while the boy was interrogated at the sheriff's office. Later, when both statements were compared, they were remarkably similar. Perhaps too similar, deputies thought, almost as if the stories had been prepared and practiced in advance.

At dawn on the next day, the boy met two county policemen in the Matthiessen parking lot and led them to the scene of the crime. The park was chilly and empty as the trio tramped through the woods damp from dew. Confused as to the attack's exact location, the boy ran ahead of the officers and was partially hidden from their view for a few seconds. "Over here," he called. The boy stood pointing to scraps of torn

clothes and fishing line lying in the dirt when the deputies caught up with him. They simply nodded and repeated the same questions that had been asked the previous night.

Although it was never proven in a court of law, the two victims later claimed that they were asked and did submit to a lie-detector examination. The La Salle County Sheriff's "lie-box" was a crude instrument designed primarily to scare the testee rather than to inform the police. Officers denied that such a test was ever given to the couple, despite the fact it was standard procedure for the department at the time.

Days later, regardless of the

The murder trial was held at the **La Salle County Courthouse** in downtown **Ottawa**.

young couple's apparent stark terror at the county jail that Sunday night, the accuracy of their separate statements and the remaining evidence found at the park, the boy and girl were astonished when the La Salle County deputies said that they didn't believe the attack took place at all.

The officers maintained that the boy had most likely thrown the strips of clothing and fishing line down when he ran ahead of the investigating policemen on the trail that cold morning. They bluntly informed the couple that they had heard that "rape" story in the past and would not waste any of the county's time and money on a worthless investigation. Humiliated in front of family and friends, the couple bitterly returned to their own lives.

They never dated again.

Word of the attack and the police refusal of continuing the probe quickly spread through the girl's small high school, adding further degradation for her. The tortured victim soon confided her story to the only woman instructor in the school, Sue Ocepeck. The shocked teacher could hardly believe that the local authorities refused to investigate the apparent crime. Sharing tears with her student, the young instructor told her the police probably wouldn't do anything about the attacker until he killed someone.

It was to be conjectured much later that if the police had believed the couple's story, the Starved Rock murders might have never occurred.

From the fall of 1959, the tragic tale next moved to Saturday, March 12, 1960, two days before the doomed Riverside women arrived in La Salle County.

Carrie Smith's* feet were still cold in her boots from a morning of sledding on the Starved Rock slopes when she left the lodge with her 12-year-old daughter and friend, Sharon Taylor.* Stuffed from a big lunch, the three had decided to walk off the meal with a hike to one of the park's picturesque canyons. Without discussion, they trudged down the slippery path that wound into St. Louis Canyon. Forgetting their hectic Chicago lives for the moment, the two women and the child enjoyed the mildness of the day and the beauty of the park. Although muddy in places, the hike along the path went quickly and they soon found themselves awestruck before the spectacular icefall at the canyon's end. The women wished aloud that they should have remembered to bring a camera to capture the scene.

*(Not their real names)

84

At right, convicted killer **Chester Otto Weger** maintains his innocence in **La Salle County's** most infamous murder case from inside Stateville Penitentiary in Joliet. Weger remains imprisoned serving a life sentence for the crime. Above, the shackled Weger poses with fellow deputies **Bill Dummett** and **Wayne Hess** and **Sheriff Ray Eutsey** during the highly publicized re-enactment of the murders in St. Louis Canyon on the day of his confession, November 17, 1960.

"Isn't it marvelous to be here out of season with no one to bother you," Carrie said, gazing up at the glittering sheet of ice. "And it is just a perfect day."

After a few minutes, the child and adults turned to leave the canyon and were surprised to see a man in front of them blocking the path out. Carrie became afraid. She did not understand why, nor could she later explain her feeling. She did wonder why they hadn't spotted the man before on the trail.

The stranger was the first to speak. "What time is it?"

"Well, judging from the sky, it must be in the neighborhood of four o'clock," Carrie answered.

The man walked closer to the trio and asked, "How do you get out of here?" He seemed to be studying them.

The question struck both adults as strange. When one goes into a box canyon, it's logical that there is only one way out, they both thought. "We are leaving," Carrie told her daughter and friend. She motioned to the stranger indicating the way out, and they nervously followed him back up the trail. About halfway to the lodge, the man mysteriously vanished into the woods. Continuing their hike, Sharon nudged her friend and whispered, "That was certainly an odd, creepy experience."

Upon their safe arrival at the inn, the two friends discussed the encounter at length. Both agreed that they felt the man meant to do them some harm and believed the only reason he didn't was because the child was with them. Having no crime to report, the women did not inform the police. Instead, they hurriedly packed and left the park for a quick ride home.

Two days later, March 14, three women stood admiring the same icefall in St. Louis Canyon. They were the middle-aged wives of a banker, a corporation attorney and a telephone company executive.

Struggling with the unfamiliar controls on her friend's camera, Lillian Oetting snapped color slides of the scene. The woman didn't notice that she had neglected to wind the film completely to the next frame after each shot. A few seconds later, they started back up the trail. A few minutes later, they were dead.

Mrs. Oetting had promised to telephone her husband that night so he could relate any news to the other spouses. When she failed to call, George Oetting placed a person-to-person call for his wife to Starved Rock Lodge. Desk personnel told the operator that the woman could not be located. Oetting, surmising that the women may have gone out someplace, was positive his wife would call him in the morning. Unconcerned, he went to bed.

Tuesday morning came and went before Oetting called the lodge again seeking to speak to his wife. The inn employee answering the call mistakenly told the worried husband that the three women had been seen at breakfast and were merely out of the lodge at that time. Reassured, Oetting relaxed.

That night, an intense winter storm struck at the heart of the Illinois Valley. In St. Louis Canyon several inches of snow slowly covered up footprints, bloodstains and other vital evidence around three cold bodies. The near-blizzard conditions continued all night, piling huge snow drifts throughout the park.

"I was framed."

Chester Otto Weger

George Oetting tried again to talk with his wife on Wednesday morning and once more, neither she nor her companions could be located. At his insistence, lodge workers entered Mrs. Oetting's room and returned with chilling news. The bags and the beds in the quiet room were untouched. A quick check of the parking lot revealed that the snow-covered station wagon had also not been moved. Shocked, Oetting realized his wife and the others could have been missing for more than 40 hours.

Oetting hurriedly phoned his longtime friend, Virgil W. Peterson, operating director of the Chicago Crime Commission. Upon hearing the news, Peterson contacted the state police and other area law enforcement agencies. Within minutes, word of the missing women reached the La Salle County Sheriff's office. Sheriff Ray Eutsey immediately organized several search parties and left with them for the park.

Bill Danley, a reporter for the local newspaper, the Daily News-Tribune, was finishing his last story for that day's edition when a telephone tip about the disappearances came into the newsroom. Grabbing a camera, Danley left and drove cautiously over the snow-packed roads toward the park. On the way the reporter speculated that perhaps the women might have slipped on the snow and fallen together off one of the many dangerous canyon trails or maybe they had simply left the park for unknown reasons. In no way did Danley suspect what he was about to witness.

Reaching the park's west entrance, Danley noticed a boy racing across an icy ravine toward the road. He drove to a small parking area just south of the entrance to find several other youths shouting that they had found three bodies.

Recognizing the boys as members of the nearby Illinois Youth Commission Forestry Camp where he had once led an Explorer Post, the reporter quickly questioned the group and followed them to the park's nearby storage garage. Once there, they contacted the waiting police officials now at the lodge and then Danley called the News-Tribune office to report the murders. In a matter of minutes, the Associated Press flashed the news across its wires.

Afterward, Danley said he was very confident that the boys were entirely capable of determining whether the women had been killed or had fallen to their deaths from the top of the canyon. And, as he followed the long procession of law officials and park rangers into the canyon, the newsman soon found that his instincts were correct.

Those walking ahead of Danley rounded a curve in the snowy trail and abruptly halted in their own tracks.

There, lying side-by-side, were the mutilated bodies of the three women. They were lying on their backs under a small ledge, their lower clothing torn away and legs open. Each had been clubbed viciously about the head. Two of the bodies were tied together with heavy white twine. All of the corpses were covered with blood and their exposed limbs discolored with bruises.

Detectives from the state police investigation bureau soon arrived and began a search of the immediate area. Except for the floor of the overhang where the bodies were discovered, the entire canyon was covered with more than six inches of snow. Carefully, the snow was removed, exposing signs of a violent struggle. Barely 10 feet away from the victims, Mrs. Murphy's Argus C-3 camera was uncovered under the snow. Its leather case was smeared with blood and the strap was broken. In the same vicinity, a shattered pair of binoculars, also blood-covered, was exposed.

Cold from his quick hike into the canyon, La Salle County State's Attorney Harland Warren wandered around the crime scene with other investigating officers. Pushing the snow aside with his foot, he bumped his boot into a frozen tree limb that was streaked in blood. With the victims' head wounds etched into his memory, he surmised that the broken branch was the murder weapon. As more of the fresh snow was brushed away, police found that much of the old snow beneath to be blood-soaked. This led to the speculation that the women were bludgeoned to death further back in the canyon and then dragged for some obscure reason into the enclosure.

Hours later, while the detectives milled around the crime scene, two men approached slowly from the mouth of the canyon's entrance. The silent men, each dressed in dark topcoats, walked directly up to the still-uncovered bodies and stared at the carnage. "God, my God!" one of the men cried as his hands covered his face. "How could they have done this?!" He broke into sobs and fell into the arms of his companion who also began to cry. The two men stood shock-still for a minute. Then they turned and, without a word to or from anyone watching them, helped each other back up the slippery trail.

Police and park officers whispered quietly as the men disappeared over a ridge. Their guesses were correct. The two crying men were Robert Lindquist and R. W. Murphy, husbands of the slain women.

Sheriff Eutsey and State's Atty. Warren agreed that the bodies would remain untouched in the canyon until the pathologists arrived from Bloomington and state crime lab personnel came from Springfield. The long, cold vigil lasted until late that night when, aided by portable lanterns and electric torches, authorities removed the victims on cloth stretchers.

The bodies were taken to the Hulse Funeral Home in Ottawa, where an extensive autopsy was performed on each of them. And although it was visibly evident at the scene that the women were molested, no evidence of rape was found, possibly due to the length of time the remains had been in freezing conditions or the limitations of 1960 medical techniques.

Following an analysis of stomach contents, the time of death was placed sometime in the middle of the afternoon the day the women arrived in the park. This was confirmed by the known fact that the victims had lunch in the inn around 1 p.m.

Robbery was almost immediately dismissed as a motive because the three dead friends had left their handbags and cash in the lodge and the jewelry on their bodies, on first inspection, appeared untouched.

The first break in the case, which was quickly announced in sensationalized front-page headlines across the nation, came following the processing of the color slide film found in the Murphy camera. Mrs. Oetting had shot five color transparencies on three frame lengths of film. Despite the overlapping exposures, three photographs were clearly enhanced by experts.

The first slide showed Mrs. Lindquist and Mrs. Murphy smiling at a site near the lodge. The next one captured the same two friends near the edge of another canyon top along the winding trail. The last photo was a picture of Mildred Lindquist in front of the St. Louis Canyon icefall. Presumably, due to the nearby location of the crime scene, the last exposure was thought to have been taken just minutes before the killer (or killers) struck.

Inexplicably, authorities soon announced that a strange shadow in the background of the last photo might in fact be the murderer, photographed before he attacked. Gaining access to the photo, reporter Bill Danley saw no human shadow in the photo and Eastman Kodak experts quickly set the record straight. The shadow was nothing more than one of the women partially hidden in the double exposure.

At this point, the probe began to wander. State's Atty. Warren, a conscientious and popular public servant, was technically in charge, but the state police maintained their authority in the case because the murders were committed on state property. The first major dispute between the county prosecutor and the state police came with the theory that the crime had been committed by Chicago gangsters. The hit men, it was conjectured by state investigators, had resorted to the murders to get "even" with Chicago Commissioner Peterson, a close friend to all three families.

Warren immediately dismissed this idea because he found it improbable that professional killers would travel nearly 100 miles for such a job without bringing along some type of weapon. Frustrated, the prosecutor was in a bind. He had to rely on the state police because La Salle County authorities had no experience dealing with a crime of that magnitude.

State cops began their investigation with intense questioning of the nearly 50 men and women who were either guests at the lodge or employees of the park. Each of them was subjected to a polygraph examination a few days after the bodies were discovered. Everyone passed.

Meanwhile, as the detectives were scrutinizing the crime site for any possible clues, Sue Ocepeck was thinking about her student/friend. She thought about the attack that the girl and her boyfriend reported. The high school teacher also thought about the police who hadn't believed their story. She had read the published accounts of the Starved Rock murders and couldn't help noticing the similarity between the two crimes. The attack came within the same general area. The victims in both cases were tied up. Clothing was also ripped in both instances and robbery seemed not the primary motive. The devoted teacher could not sit idly by. The suspicions nagged at her conscience. She decided that she had to do something. So late one night, Mrs. Ocepeck wrote a letter to the La Salle County Sheriff's Department. In it, she asked the same questions that had been bothering her. She waited for the police to make the next move.

Fear that began with the announcement of the crime increased at an alarming rate each day as it became apparent there would be no quick solution. Doors that were never bolted were now locked tight. Local hardware stores had a run on locks. The number of overnight guests at the park's lodge dropped dramatically. Motorists even went miles out of their way just to avoid driving near the canyon entrance.

However, there were several institutions which prospered from this fear, namely state-wide newspapers and other media organizations. Each day's editions of Chicago metropolitan newspapers carried banner headlines recounting the slow progress of the murder investigation. Reporters from the wire services, television and such national magazines as Life and Newsweek soon replaced late winter vacationers at the lodge.

Competition for breaking stories in the case was fierce, despite the fact there was little happening in the first few days of the probe. Chicago newsmen, enjoying the comfort of the lodge with their wives, would make bold headlines out of the simplest of police news releases. Lodge employees would laugh as they watched the metropolitan reporters swoop down on the local papers after copies were delivered to the lodge. With the rural published accounts in their hands, they would then file their "own" stories in long distance calls to their big-city editors.

Besides selling newspapers, the headlines also increased pressure on law enforcement agencies to solve the case. The intense clamor for a solution had an effect inside Harland Warren's county office. The state's attorney was doing everything in his power to end the mystery, but he did not welcome the additional stress, especially in an election year. His opponents began to shout charges of incompetency, but Warren had no choice. He continued to wait for further developments from state officials.

In the interim, employers of the mourning husbands offered a total of $30,000 in rewards for information leading to a conviction. Another $5,000 was put up by Nicholas Spiros, concessionaire at the lodge. Authorities had no idea whether this offer of money would be a help or a curse in the search.

Money was also becoming a question on a different front. The La Salle County Board of Supervisors substantially reduced the special financial requests of both prosecutor Warren and Sheriff Eutsey to cover the soaring expenses of the manhunt. The board felt that the state should pay the expenses since the crime was committed on state property. A special session of the county board to discuss the investigation costs resulted in a shouting match between the supervisors and the county law officials. One board member blasted Warren, stating "We are operating a home for unemployed attorneys on the fourth floor (Warren's courthouse office)!"

Newsmen assigned to the murder case were struck

Spectacular icefalls throughout **Starved Rock State Park** attract thousands of hikers each winter season.

at the contrast between the bickering of the board and the thought-to-be competent detective work being done on the search. Editorials in local papers demanded more cooperation within the agencies sworn to protect and service the frightened citizens of La Salle County.

As a direct result of those newspapers' articles, confidence appeared to be restored somewhat in state officials who maintained that the crime would soon be solved. Only days later, a scandal of professional blundering destroyed that confidence.

The scandal began quietly when a routine check of personal items found on the victims revealed that a small diamond ring was missing from Mrs. Oetting's effects. Jumping on a possible significant lead, authorities sent out detectives and notices to Illinois pawnshops in a search for the piece of jewelry. Many man-hours were put into the search across the state.

However, when the state crime lab in Springfield returned the blood-soaked clothing back to Ottawa a month later, a county deputy found the missing ring inside what was later identified as Mrs. Oetting's glove. Speculation was that the victim had simply slipped the ring off her finger sometime during the confrontation before her death. Precious time and money had been wasted on the false clue.

Journalists publicized the "goof" with brutal spitefulness, naming the overworked, under-manned and poorly-equipped criminal lab an embarrassment to the state. Unit superintendent James Christensen defended his staff but, despite dozens of years of noteworthy law enforcement service, he finally resigned under the burst of public and private indignation.

County authorities, plagued by the fear of what other mistakes might have been made by the apparently careless state agency, quietly sent all of the crime's physical evidence to the Michigan state crime laboratory for reexamination. The shame of the "missing ring" scandal ultimately moved then Gov. Otto Kerner and state legislators to increase funding for the investigative unit. The upgrading eventually transformed the crime unit into one of the country's most respected research institutions.

The summer of 1960 was especially hot for Harland Warren.

Months crawled by and all possible clues led to only dead ends in the baffling case. Authorities even contacted Mrs. Ocepeck to discuss her letter. After their short interview, the teacher never heard from anyone about the reported 1959 rape and robbery again.

In August, Warren decided that he had taken enough abuse from his critics for not finding a solution to the murders. He was a prosecutor, not a detective. Frustrated, however, he accepted the challenge. Transforming from state's attorney to investigator, he gathered up all the existing evidence and shut himself up in a small room. Now what was here, the lawyer asked himself, that the murderer left behind at the scene of the crime?

The obvious and only answer was the twine which the killer had used to bind his victims.

Warren had never played detective in all his years as the head La Salle County prosecutor, but he saw no alternative. Reaching into his own pocket, he bought a simple $80 microscope and studied the cord intently. He discovered that there were two kinds of twine used-one was 20-ply and the other 12-ply. Somehow, Warren knew, he had to start with these small facts.

The county official also knew that he needed help. He chose two men to work with him, not out of his public courthouse office but rather out of his nearby private law agency. No longer satisfied with the questionable work of state detectives, Warren wanted these men to report to him and him alone.

He handpicked county deputies Bill Dummett and Wayne Hess, two men he considered trustworthy and intelligent. These friends would not jeopardize the inquiry by feeding information to the newspapers which was more than could be said for others involved in the case.

Dummett, who died in 1982, started in police work on the county jail switchboard. Hess, also deceased, was a low-key, thoughtful man, who lived with his family on a farm near Utica close to the scene of the crime. Neither man had done any serious sleuthing, but each quickly accepted the prosecutor's assignment.

Setting the twine question aside for the moment, Warren began to study the color transparencies found in Mrs. Murphy's camera. He realized that it was scientifically possible to establish the point in time when a photo was exposed. Consulting with an expert from Ohio State University, calculations were made based on heights of objects and length of shadows on the film. The expert pinpointed the time of one of the transparencies at 2:33 p.m. on March 14, 1960. Comparing that time into the geography of the locale and the known route that the women had to hike, Warren fixed the time of the murders at between 3:15 and 3:30 p.m. This was far more precise than the time set in the autopsy reports based on the food digested in the women's stomachs.

Having the time established, Warren's attention turned back to the twine found on the bodies. The logical place to start a search for the cord's origin was at Starved Rock Lodge itself, so one night in September 1960, he met the concessionaire at the inn's kitchen. Within minutes and without much difficulty, Warren found two different types of twine, each used in wrapping food, which ultimately matched the number of strands, 12 and 20, used in the murders. Deputies Dummett and Hess, using lodge purchasing records, soon tracked down the twine's manufacturer. The firm's officials identified the murder cord as twine produced in their plant and without question, taken from the ball found in the kitchen.

WEGER GETS LIFE AS BIRTHDAY GIFT
La Salle-Peru Daily News-Tribune headline

Just as Warren had always suspected, the killer had to either work at or have access to the park's lodge.

Faced with the fact that all lodge employees had passed polygraph tests earlier in the investigation, the state's attorney, remembering the foul-ups the state police had made on the evidence examination, now thought that their lie-detection efforts might also have been erroneous. Boldly, he decided it was time to run some of his own tests. Hiring a specialist from the John Reid Institute, a nationally prominent Chicago polygraph firm, Warren recalled all lodge employees who worked the week of the murders. One by one, the confused personnel paraded through lie tests in one of the small log cabins near the lodge. The first dozen men and women subjected to the analysis were quickly cleared and it seemed for a while that the desperate detectives might be wasting their time. Then Dummett brought in an ex-dishwasher, Chester Otto Weger. Completing the exam, the polygraph pro's face was pale as he watched the slight man walk away from the cabin. After months of endless leads and wasted investigations, the technician Stephen J. Kindig ended all doubt for Warren and his two deputies at that moment. "There's your man," he whispered.

Weger, 21, was a slight, short man with a wife and two small children. He had worked at the park until that summer when he went into business with his father as a painter. Dummett remembered the young man from an earlier state police report. Inexplicably and without any protest, Weger began a long period of nearly unbelievable cooperation with the investigators. He surrendered a piece of his buckskin jacket to the authorities so they could have some suspicious "dark blotches" analyzed. The stains, first reported in the state police's initial investigation, had been dismissed earlier as "probably animal blood." Previously, Weger had lived with his family near the back end of Matthiessen Park where he often went on long walks or hunted animals throughout the dense forests. There had been no reason to question Weger further about the stains once he had explained that to state detectives. The small piece was forwarded to the state lab.

Warren, who wanted to be positive in the direction of the probe, had his deputies ask Weger to go to Chicago for a battery of lie-tests to confirm the validity of the reexamination. Weger agreed without hesitation. It was as if he welcomed the attention without fear of its implications.

Again, the former dishwasher flunked each exam.

Realizing that the polygraph examinations were inadmissible in court, Warren began to gather the proof he needed to arrest Weger for the brutal crime. Checking the lodge's time-card records, the prosecutor found that the suspect was off work between 2 and 5 p.m. on the murder date. Warren knew that was plenty of time for Weger to follow the women into the canyon, kill them and return to the inn to work the dinner shift, Warren thought.

Next, upon hearing from the lab that the jacket piece was too small for an accurate analysis, Dummett coaxed Weger into giving him the jacket for more tests. Again, Weger agreed without hesitation. The detective sent the coat to the FBI offices in Washington. Less than a week passed before federal technicians replied with a report that sent the investigators' hopes soaring. Though the scientific abilities of even the government research facilities were limited in 1960 when compared to modern-day laboratories, the federal agency determined the blotches on the jacket to be human blood which could not be typed. In addition, they stated that the stains came from flying blood, as if it had been splattered on the coat. It was definitely not blood from a hunting trip or a simple nosebleed, the report concluded.

Warren, believing to have his first physical piece of evidence against Weger, requested continuous state police surveillance of Weger. The county prosecutor wanted to be sure that no harm came to anyone else as he compiled the case for the grand jury.

It was at this point, as Dummett checked further into Weger's past, that the deputy suddenly recalled the 1959 rape/robbery story told by two teenagers. The deputy was stunned to realize that Weger's Oglesby home was just a few hundred yards away from the reported attack. With Warren's approval, Dummett and Hess approached the young female victim with a stack of mug shots. Sorting through them slowly, she screamed at the face of Chester Weger.

With that positive identification, Warren could easily have ordered Weger arrested, but a different problem was at hand. Spending all his time and energy on the evidence search, the state's attorney had worked very little on his own campaign for reelection. If he booked Weger on the rape and murder charges before the election, Warren knew the defense would call such a move political and designed primarily to retain his $9,500-a-year job.

Confident of his record, Harland Warren decided to stand on his past history of cleaning out the rampant gambling and prostitution houses from La Salle County during his eight years in office. The Democratic opponent, Robert E. Richardson, continued to blast Warren for his "bungling" of the Starved Rock case, noting the silence coming out of the courthouse as the election approached.

Out of almost 60,000 votes, Warren lost by nearly 3,500.

Naturally disappointed by the election results, the defeated state's attorney felt better after he learned that a tip had checked out successfully. Carrie Smith and a friend, Sharon Taylor, had reported the story of their strange encounter the weekend before the murders near the beginning of the investigation. Searching through police mug shots, the two women recognized their mysterious stranger as Chester Weger. Their identification placed the county's prime suspect at the scene of the crime (even though it was days earlier). Warren felt he could wait no longer. He wanted to face his outspoken critics with an arrest that he felt sure would eventually lead to a conviction. He realized that his case was not as solid as he might have hoped for, but the prosecutor gambled that once Weger was faced with the mounting evidence, the young man might confess.

On Nov. 17, Warren obtained an arrest warrant for Weger for the 1959 rape/robbery and ordered Hess and Dummett to pick him up. Careful plans were discussed in which the attorney instructed his men to interrogate Weger before confronting him with the murder charges.

Walking directly past the state police surveillance team in front of Weger's La Salle apartment, the two deputies first told them and then Weger that they simply wanted to take him in for more questions. They made no mention of the arrest warrants waiting at the courthouse. Once back in Ottawa, the two country cops faced their suspect with the rape/robbery warrants and began to press him on the murder case. The questions continued past midnight.

Weary of the policemen's relentless inquiry and distressed about his arrest, Weger suddenly stopped in mid-answer and asked to see his family. A patrol car was dispatched to his parent's Oglesby home and his mother and father were rushed to the court-house. Dummett and Hess gave Weger a few minutes alone with them.

"I did it."
Chester Otto Weger

In his official statement taken the next day, Deputy Hess said, "When Bill (Dummett) stepped out of the back room in the state's attorney office to show Mr. and Mrs. Weger to the door so they could go home..., I could see something was bothering Chester."

"I said, 'Chester, why don't you tell me about it? There are just two of us here... Just tell me about it." He said, 'All right, I did it.' He said, 'I got scared. I tried to grab their pocketbook (which was actually the Argus camera), they fought and I hit them.'"

Minutes later, a court reporter was summoned to the courthouse where a confession was transcribed and each page was signed by Weger. After nearly eight months of searching, the accused killer was in custody.

During the confession, when asked why he had apparently dragged the bodies into the overhang in

St. Louis Canyon, Weger said he had spotted a small airplane flying low over the park. Weger said that he thought it could be a state police plane and so, moved the bodies to hide them from an aerial view.

A few days later, this flight over Starved Rock was confirmed by both the plane's pilot and his log book.

Weger confessed several more times to the murders on the next day and even reenacted the crime in the canyon for a host of policemen and reporters. However, following his first meeting with a court-appointed attorney, he changed his story, stating that he was innocent to any and all charges. Weger maintained that Dummett and Hess had threatened him with a gun that night in the courthouse and, to save his life, he falsely accepted and signed their composed confession. The prisoner told his lawyer that it was Dummett who fed him the information about the plane over the canyon.

"I was in Oglesby at the time of the murders," Weger insisted.

Selection of a jury, which took almost two weeks and involved the examination of more than 359 veniremen, began on January 30, 1961, and the trial subsequently was called to order on February 3. Richardson, the newly sworn-in state's attorney, and his first assistant, Anthony Raccuglia, together pleaded the county's case against Weger in the courtroom of Judge Leonard Hoffman. The trial, which attracted national attention, was the first criminal case either of the county attorneys had prosecuted. The suggested idea of appointing Warren as special prosecutor had been dismissed earlier by the legal team. The ex-state's attorney would have to watch from the sidelines.

Surprisingly, Richardson and Raccuglia decided to face Weger in court for only one of the three murders. The reasoning was that in the event of a mistrial, an innocent verdict or an unsatisfactory sentence, the attorneys could try the man for the second and again for the third killing.

They sought the death penalty.

On March 4, almost exactly a year after the Starved Rock murders were committed, Chester Weger was pronounced guilty in causing Lillian Oetting's death. The La Salle Daily News-Tribune, in a banner headline, told the story: WEGER GETS LIFE AS BIRTHDAY GIFT. The imposed sentence of life imprisonment to the state penitentiary had coincided with his 22nd birthday.

Following the jury's dismissal by Judge Hoffman, reporters rushed up to the 12 men and women to ask if any of them knew that a life sentence under Illinois law meant Weger would be eligible for parole consideration in just a few years. Most of the jurors were shocked and said no. Some were quoted as saying that if they had known about the parole possibilities, they would have voted for the electric chair. Apparently, little knowledge of Illinois criminal procedure and the fact that the prosecution could not by law mention it, had most probably saved Weger's life.

Months later, Richardson, reportedly under financial pressure from the county board and the urge to get the matter behind him, decided to let the life sentence stand as the final punishment for Weger. He did not proceed with any of the other charges against Weger, including the Matthiessen Park rape/robbery. That decision infuriated the youngsters and their parents who had already suffered at the hands of county authorities.

The convicted prisoner was incarcerated in Stateville Penitentiary in Joliet while his attorney, the late John McNamara of Marseilles, tried unsuccessfully for years to free his client.

On July 18, 1963, the Starved Rock triple murder reward funds were distributed by the executors to seven parties, with the lion's share, $11,500, awarded to Harland Warren. Shares of $5,500 each went to county officers Dummett and Hess, along with Stephen J. Kindig, operator of the tale-telling lie test. Teacher Sue Ocepeck received $5,000 for her informational letter, and $2,675 to Carrie Smith and Sharon Taylor for their identification of Weger.

At the time of this writing in 1997, Weger remains in prison. From his cell at Canton's medium security Illinois River Correctional Center, the middle-aged man continues to maintain his innocence. Despite regular parole hearings since his first one in 1972, Weger does not know when , if ever, he will be released. Suffering from failing eyesight, he spends much of his day reading his oversized-print Bible and listening to the radio. "I was framed," Weger maintains. "People in La Salle County know that, so does Warren and so did Hess and Dummett."

Maud Powell

Born in 1867, a time when Peru, Illinois was considered part of the "western frontier," **Maud Powell** became America's first great female violin virtuoso of international acclaim. She lived the first three years of her life in a two-story brick house on Bluff Street in Peru and was called a music prodigy as a child by many famous masters.

The renowned violinist studied and performed music around the world, setting new standards for classic concert performances.

In 1910, at the height of her career, the musician returned to her birthplace for a hometown recital. Local residents cheered her performance.

She was also an educator who encouraged young music students and spoke out in favor of hiring talented women musicians on an equal basis with men to perform in orchestras.

Maud Powell died of a heart attack in 1920.

To honor their most famous former resident, the people of Peru dedicated a stunning statue of Maud, violin in hand, on July 1, 1995 in the city's East Plaza. The monument celebrates her lifelong commitment to music and her successful struggle in breaking down the established barriers to women performing in the arts.

101

Lightning from a fierce spring storm splits the night sky and silhouettes the brick clock tower of **La Salle-Peru High School**. Completed in 1898, the high school's classic appearance is unique to **Illinois Valley** architecture.

THE NIGHT LINDBERGH CRASHED

T he year was 1926.

Dense fog a thousand feet thick formed a blanket over northern Illinois on the night of September 16. Lost in the clear, black sky above, an airmail plane pilot strained his eyes, desperately searching for an opening as his engine sputtered out of fuel. Silently, the airplane began to fall into the dark.

The pilot was Charles A. Lindbergh.

Five months earlier, Lindbergh, 24, then an unknown barnstormer, had flown the first airmail route from St. Louis to Chicago. His young aviation business welcomed new U.S. government mail contracts as it provided many gypsy pilots with their first regular flying jobs.

Employed by a small Chicago aircraft company, Lindbergh had charted a 285-mile route between the two major Midwestern cities, including gas and mail pickup stops at Springfield and Peoria. Along with several other company fliers, he was determined to improve airmail efficiency over train mail routes.

The **Jason DeBolt** farmhouse outside **Wedron** where airmail pilot **Charles Lindbergh** was welcomed overnight after his near-fatal crash in 1926.

To accomplish this goal, flights were regularly scheduled even though proper weather information was not always provided and ground lights were simply not available at many landing fields. If a pilot had to land at night, he had to first drop a tiny parachute flare in order to light his way for a landing. Each aircraft in Lindbergh's tiny company carried such a flare.

The flight from St. Louis that September evening was proceeding normally for Lindbergh as he cruised north over the Illinois plains following his brief Peoria stopover. There was no weather service to warn him of the approaching fog bank that was rolling south over his base strip at Chicago's Maywood Field (now O'Hare Airport).

Realizing that the overdue pilot may be in trouble, searchlights, as well as huge oil drum fires, were lit along the landing strip in the hope that Lindbergh might be able to catch a glimpse of them through the thick cover.

The lost pilot never saw them.

Instead, Lindbergh turned his plane toward the south, seeking a pocket clear of fog. He was not overly concerned because he estimated that his craft had enough fuel for another hour of flying, not counting the additional emergency tank. He was more than confident that a field would be found in plenty of time.

What the young pilot didn't know was that, due to a leak found sometime before his original takeoff, the airplane's usual 110-gallon tank had been replaced in St. Louis with an 85-gallon tank. Therefore, it was completely unexpected when his engine suddenly stopped. Lindbergh immediately switched to the emergency tank, which he knew would give the plane another 20 minutes of flight. Now, peering down into the darkness, he began to worry. Later, in his official report, he wrote, "I decided to leave the ship as soon as the reserve tank was exhausted. I tried to get the mail pit open with the idea of throwing out the mail sacks, and then jumping, but was unable to open the front buckle."

Searching, Lindbergh saw a faint light on the ground, but soon lost it. He glided down to 1,200 feet and released his only flare. It disappeared without revealing a trace of the ground. His fuel and time were running out.

Climbing again, the plane reached almost 5,000 feet. Again, the engine began to sputter. Then it went silent. Wasting no time, Lindbergh leaped over the side and pulled his parachute's ripcord. It opened quietly above him. With a small flashlight in his hand, he floated in the night and waited to hit the ground.

His troubles, however, were not over.

Lindbergh's report explained: "When I had jumped, it (the engine) had stopped dead and I had neglected to cut the switches. Apparently when the ship nosed down, an additional supply of gasoline drained to the carburetor." He heard the engine, cranked to life by a spinning propeller, coming toward him. The pilotless aircraft began to circle the dangling parachutist.

Floating helplessly, Lindbergh got the unpleasant feeling that the plane was playing cat-and-mouse with him: "Soon (the plane) came into sight, about a quarter of a mile away, and headed in the general direction of my parachute. The plane was making a left spiral of about a mile in diameter and passed approximately 300 yards away from me... I counted five spirals, each one a little further away than the last, before it reached the top of the fog bank."

Hundreds of feet below Lindbergh and his parachute, Jason DeBolt awoke around 10 p.m. to the sound of a plane over his farmhouse outside the small village of Wedron. Sitting up in bed, he heard the plane nose-dive into the ground. Quickly dressing in the dark, the farmer jumped in his car and drove to a field south of his house. There he found the wreckage of a crumpled aircraft that had mowed down several

The quiet and shy pilot who came to be known world-wide as **"Lucky Lindy"** was certainly fortunate to survive a plane crash outside **Wedron**, Illinois only months before he landed in Paris as an international hero. **Charles Lindbergh** stands next to his smashed mail route aircraft before taking his postal delivery by train to Chicago in September 1926.

rows of his corn crop. It had narrowly missed another farmhouse and had skidded 80 yards through the corn. DeBolt, examining the crash and the surrounding area, found the mailbags, but no sign of a pilot. He rushed back home and called the sheriff's department.

Meanwhile, Francis and Ella Johnson, who lived in the same vicinity, had also heard the plane crash. Together, they set out in their Maxwell automobile to search out the accident scene.

Still up in the sky, Lindbergh, realizing that he was rapidly approaching the ground, crossed his legs to keep from straddling a branch or wire in his descent. Abruptly, he saw the earth just an instant before he slammed into a cornfield. The chute, supported by the stalks, hung over him like an umbrella. The uninjured pilot gathered up the cloth and started down the corn row. Once on the country road, he saw the headlights of the Johnsons' car and flagged them down. They took him to their home while he calmly explained what had happened. When they tried to call the sheriff, the community operator, Esther Barr, told them where to find the plane.

> **"I could fly all night... like the moon."**
> Charles Lindbergh

By the time Lindbergh got to the scene, several other area residents had gathered around the plane. There was even an astute photographer present to record the lanky pilot at the scene of the accident. DeBolt and his neighbors helped the mail carrier collect the pouches and place them in a car. The bags were taken to the Ottawa Post Office and put aboard the next train to Chicago.

The DeBolt family welcomed the exhausted pilot into their home for that night and also the next, following a day dedicated to the examination of the destroyed plane. Before his death, Jason DeBolt remembered Lindbergh as quiet, gracious and surprisingly unbothered by the harrowing near tragedy, according to the farmer's sister, Hazel Wiley of Wedron. She said that her brother drove the lucky pilot to Ottawa to catch a train on September 18. Sometime after he left, the DeBolt family received a thank-you note from "Lindy" along with $10 enclosed for their kindness and trouble.

The airplane crash was reported in the press, but as if to insure that Lindbergh remained completely obscure, news stories listed his name as Carl Lindberg.

Returning immediately to the air company, Lindbergh resumed the mail route with his fellow pilots. However, less than two months later, on the night of November 4, a plane piloted by Lindbergh ran out of fuel in a blinding sleet storm outside Peoria. Once again, he bailed out and landed unhurt. The blond flyer became a prominent member of the "Caterpillar Club," a fictitious organization invented by pilots who had become "butterflies" by descending to earth in parachutes. Although the two Lindbergh crashes cost his company half its fleet, the airflight business continued delivering the mail all that long winter.

In retrospect, the St. Louis-to-Chicago airflights were important beyond the simple fact of validating Lindbergh as lucky, for it was on these routes that he dreamed of much larger and vastly more important accomplishments. He wondered how far he could fly if the plane was loaded down with more gas rather than letters and packages. Often on those flights, the aviator wished he could skip Chicago and fly nonstop to New York. He thought of the constant advances in airplane technology and soon became confident that a plane, flying at a low speed, could stay aloft for days. He also thought of the $25,000 prize that had been offered by New York hotel magnate, Raymond Orteig, to the first aviator to fly straight through from New York to France. "I could fly all night, like the moon," he told himself. "Possibly— I could fly nonstop between New York and Paris!" The bold thought both startled and excited him.

The dream, possibly born on a lonely, Midwest mail route, became a reality a few months later in May 1927. For that epochal trans-Atlantic flight, Charles A. Lindbergh, the unknown pilot, became an international hero forever. And, because the gospel of aviation was preached by a man who had captivated the entire world, the business of flying was validated forever.

Flowing water cascades from a higher lake down into the lower dells of **Matthiessen State Park** outside **Oglesby**, Illinois. The 1,938-acre park, originally called **Deer Park,** was named for the late **Frederick W. Matthiessen**, a remarkable philanthropist from **La Salle**, who first developed the area at the end of the 1800s. The retreat features seven miles of marked trails.

A powerful tugboat pushes a long barge into the navigational locks in this aerial view of **Starved Rock Dam** between **Ottawa** and **Utica**. The Starved Rock facility is one of eight similar locks along the **Illinois River Waterway** that link the Great Lakes with the Mississippi River. Maintained by the U. S. Army Corps of Engineers, the 327 mile-long waterway is tremendously important to Illinois commerce. Such vital products on coal, grain, sand, iron, steel and other chemicals are carried on the river almost daily by the slow-moving tugs.

THE DEATH OF TRADER JACK

The year was 1955.

John Spencer Redshaw was many different people. He was a husband, a father, a postmaster, a jeweler, a collector and a veteran. But to those who remember him more than 40 years after his violent death, Redshaw still is Trader Jack, perhaps the most talented businessperson north central Illinois has ever seen.

But Redshaw was also the victim of the most vicious unsolved murder in the history of Illinois' Putnam County. Ironically, it was the same unique business that made him internationally famous that eventually led to his baffling assassination.

His body, discovered on the floor of his Granville store's huge vault on September 26, 1955, had been savagely beaten and shot three times in a crime never explained.

The murdered man's saga began in the 1920s when, as a poor coal miner's son, Redshaw started to trade modest items with a shrewd and seemingly natural instinct for the better deal. His barter business boomed due to such scenarios as swapping a handful of average knives for musical instruments, musical instruments for a truckload of novelty items, novelty items for a trunkful of guns, guns for a handful of precious jewels, the jewels for rare paintings, and on and on. Actual money meant little to him and his beloved barters; he simply preferred merchandise.

Former Putnam State's Attorney W. Durley Boyle

Redshaw, once postmaster of his small village, proved that the world would truly beat a path to your door if you had something to offer, even if that door was hundreds of miles away from the nearest major metropolitan center.

Following his own method of operation, he once initiated a series of complicated trades that started with a 35mm Leica camera and ultimately wound up with a banana plantation in Central America. Old timers in Granville still spin the story of how "Trader Jack" swapped a houseboat on the Ganges River for valuable real estate in Detroit. Reports of his dealings such as those were admittedly rare. Redshaw kept the vast majority of his complex transactions secret, thus was born his legend and fortune. He eventually served as host to businesspeople from all over the world who came to his small village to deal with the master trader. Some called him "The Midwest Maharajah."

Realizing the value of personal publicity, Redshaw wore explosive-colored clothing during a period of conservative dress. His fingers were covered with dazzling jewelry which often held dozens of huge diamonds, rubies and emeralds. Even his eyeglasses bore the name "Trader Jack" engraved in pure silver on the frames.

Interviewed in the October 1945 issue of Reader's Digest, Redshaw said, "Every other business is crowded but in trading, you almost have no competition. There are billions of dollar's worth of goods lying around to be transferred by a good trader... and a good commission on each swap!"

That year, his cavernous, block-long warehouse in Granville was filled with nearly every imaginable item: vacuum cleaners, Ming vases, cases of corncob pipes, Turkish carpets, antique and modern weapons, waffles irons, clocks, leopard skins, and so on, all piled from floor to ceiling. The warehouse also held two huge vaults and several safes. Rumors around the town put Redshaw's personal wealth in excess of $2 million.

Perhaps it was just this kind of envious gossip which led to his kidnapping years before his murder.

Late in the 1930s, Redshaw was once lured out of his office by a stranger and was forced into a car filled with desperate accomplices. He was then beaten, robbed and held hostage for several hours before his captors released him. No ransom was ever demanded for or paid out.

Afterward, the flashy trader swore to all his friends and family that he would never again be taken against his will. To many customers during their marathon bargaining sessions, he would frequently reveal a big, black revolver he kept in his desk at all times.

It was business as usual for the 61-year-old man until the morning of Monday, September 26, 1955. That day, Granville resident Vivian Anderson noticed two men wearing gray hats cruising the village's narrow streets in a two-tone green Oldsmobile. Strangers rarely traveled through Granville without notice. It did turn out to be more than unfortunate that Mrs. Anderson did not get a close look at the strangers in the big car.

Norman Hoover, another villager, passed Redshaw's warehouse shortly before 10 a.m. and observed the trader at his desk. Questioned later by local authorities, Hoover could not remember whether or not the Oldsmobile was in front of the building.

Nearly two hours later, Redshaw's wife, Mary, came to the office to meet him for lunch. In the deep recess of the inner vault, she discovered the open door and the body of her husband- savagely beaten and riddled with .38 caliber bullets. Lying beside the body was a submachine gun which the trader had kept on the wall amid piles of other merchandise. It had no bullet clip in it, and detectives could not determine

The huge vault where **Trader Jack** was found murdered in 1955 remains intact today as the **Granville** Township office and library. The massive amount of goods gathered by **Redshaw** was sold by his family after his death.

whether or not the man had reached for it to protect himself. The dead man had $240 in his pocket and a massive 12-carat diamond ring on his finger when his body was found.

As the inquiry began, the green Oldsmobile was soon found three miles west of the village. It was later discovered to have been stolen in Chicago the weekend before the crime. An examination of the vehicle revealed little insight as to the identities of the killers.

Faced with few clues, Putnam County State's Attorney W. Durley Boyle initiated an intensive investigation that would ultimately consume thousand of man-hours.

Although it was at first thought that some valuable diamonds and other gems might have been stolen during the attack, Boyle could never confirm it. Redshaw had always kept the vast warehouse inventory in his head and confided his business to no one. Also, as Boyle and his detectives sifted through the huge warehouse, the prosecutor was astounded at the sheer volume of precious goods and he immediately understood that there was no way to account for any missing items.

Boyle was told that Redshaw had allowed very few people into his back vault. That fact led him to believe that the murderers might have clients the trader had met previously. Supporting that fact was the jeweler's eyepiece Redshaw had fastened to his glasses before he was shot. The attorney considered this as evidence that the victim must had examined gems in the presence of his slayers.

Various Illinois crime agencies worked with Putnam County officials in the effort to solve the case and more than 100 possible suspects were brought in for interrogations. Some were former customers, others known jewel thieves and ex-convicts.

Rumors circulated around Granville that Redshaw's business might have been part of a fencing operation, but an FBI investigation eliminated that possibility. Detectives followed many different leads and directions, all of which ended in frustration.

The case remains unsolved today.

Interviewed more than 30 years later, the viciousness of the crime lingered in the mind of former prosecutor Boyle. He referred to the case as the most brutal that he had ever connected with during his 40 years as state's attorney.

"It was definitely a professional job," Boyle said, adding that the stolen auto, the lack of witnesses and the sadistic shooting all logically pointed to a well-planned attack. "And because of the lack of any robbery evidence, even a clear motive for the slaying has never been established..." The prosecutor, a friend who had done some trading business with Redshaw himself (as did most local residents) stressed the fact that dealing in gems and guns could be a very dangerous occupation. "Somebody was out for him," Boyle concluded. "I still have hopes that someone will confess to this crime..."

Redshaw's death marked the end to his international career but did little to halt the legend that swelled following the murder. The story of his trades, so well known and yet so secretive, continues to this day with countless tales of his wheeling and dealing.

In a local newspaper editorial published shortly after the trader's funeral, it was written that the murder merely added to the mystery which surrounded Redshaw all during his life.

The truth is that neither Trader Jack's life nor death may ever be completely understood.

GATEWAY TO THE WEST

The year was 1814.

In a message to the U. S. Congress, President James Madison called for a feasibility study of building a waterway between Lake Michigan at Chicago to the Illinois River, thus allowing access to the Mississippi River for the purpose of commerce. The dream of such a new waterway, however, did not originate with that particular presidential address.

As early as the first European exploration of the upper midwest during the early 1600s by Father Pere Marquette and Louis Jolliet, the advantages of a portage became apparent to them as a "gateway to the west" and the Gulf of Mexico. Fur traders and struggling pioneers who traveled and settled along the Illinois River valley also spoke of and lobbied government offices for the construction for just such a waterway.

In the 1820s, the second decade of Illinois' statehood, the Erie Canal, a new and superior emigrant and trade route, did much to transform Chicago from a quiet trading post community to the first midwestern boomtown. Sparked by that canal's success, the Illinois General Assembly created a Canal Commission and passed bits and pieces of legislation that furthered the waterway's construction.

On July 4, 1836, the Illinois-Michigan Canal was officially started and soon became an on-again, off-again project, once shutting down for more than four years due to funding problems. Monies were funneled in from foreign and eastern investors to complete the long ditch. The 100-mile canal opened its 15 locks in 1848 and was successful for many years until the railroads slowly took both freight and passenger business away.

All commercial use of the I & M ended with the opening of the Canal's logically successor, the Illinois River Waterway.

The still waters of the **Illinois-Michigan Canal** and its adjacent towpath attract many visitors daily for a variety of recreational activities. Thanks in part to the local rotary clubs and area volunteers, a barely recognizable canal between **La Salle** and **Utica** was resculptured and filled with water in the 1970s after many decades of neglect.

President Ronald Reagan signs the **Illinois-Michigan Canal** congressional bill into law at the Chicago Conrad Hilton Hotel on August 24, 1984. The legislation mandated federal protection and funds for the historic waterway on August 24, 1984. The ceremony, attended by dozens of Illinois politicians and area residents, ended years of local effort to restore the I & M into a national landmark. Following the signing, President Reagan said that the bill would "stimulate tourism, jobs and economic growth" along the unique federal preserve. The desk on which the bill signing was held is now a permanent exhibit at the **La Salle County Historical Society Museum** in **Utica**.

A lone cabin cruiser cuts through the **Illinois River** under the sheer sandstone cliffs of **Buffalo Rock State Park** outside **Naplate**.

THE LEONORE BANK ROBBERY

T he year was 1935.

John Dillinger, the daring bank robber whose exploits created a folk legend, had been dead for nearly six months... or so the public had been told.

Born in Indianapolis, Indiana on June 22, 1903, Dillinger became perhaps the most infamous bank robber of the 20th century. He began his rise to criminal immortality after he was sent to prison for armed robbery in 1924 and served time until his parole in 1933. During the next year, Dillinger captured the nation's (as well as the Federal Bureau of Investigation's) attention as he and his bold gang held up banks across several states. The hardened criminal was captured on several occasions during that year, only to escape time after time from various law enforcement agencies. The FBI secured Dillinger's place in history by naming him "Public Enemy Number One" and offering a $20,000 reward for his capture dead or alive. As federal agents conducted a massive manhunt, the thief was lured to the Biograph Theater in Chicago on July 22, 1934 by Anna Sage, the mysterious so-called "Lady in Red." There, in ambush style, FBI agents ended the legend in a hailstorm of gunfire. Had the seemingly uncatchable, invincible Dillinger really been shot by federal agents in a dark Chicago alley? Police and other witnesses swore that he was killed. However, the

The **State Bank of Leonore** building was the starting point of a robbery which ultimately cost the lives of seven people, one a **Marshall County** Sheriff, in 1935. Long abandoned, the building was demolished several years ago. The electrocution of three men involved in the foiled crime marked the last time anyone from **La Salle County** convicted in a capital punishment trial was actually put to death.

popular notion across the country was that the country-boy bandit wasn't the same man that was ambushed and gunned down. Denials of Dillinger's death surfaced with every new bank holdup.

Legends die hard.

And although the bloody Leonore, Illinois bank robbery was not masterminded by the dead Dillinger, it was undoubtedly a product of that legend.

On the cold morning of Wednesday, January 16, 1935, the nation's attention was focused on the ongoing trial of Bruno Richard Hauptmann for the kidnapping and murder of baby Charles A. Lindbergh, Jr. The FBI's attention was on surrounding the infamous Kate "Ma" Barker gang in Oklawaha, Florida. And on the last day of his life, Charles Bundy's attention was on a mysterious black sedan parked behind the State Bank of Leonore.

The 47-year-old Bundy was the head cashier and acting president of the bank and something of a hero around the tiny village at that time. Six weeks before he bravely struck an armed bandit in the face, single-handedly preventing a robbery at his bank. Villagers were still very wary of strangers during the early days of the new year. So an unfamiliar car circling through the Leonore's narrow streets before dawn attracted special notice by the locals.

A phone call from one of those observant village residents first alerted Bundy that a suspicious vehicle was parked in back of his bank. Also, unknown to the bank clerk at that time, a small group of gun-

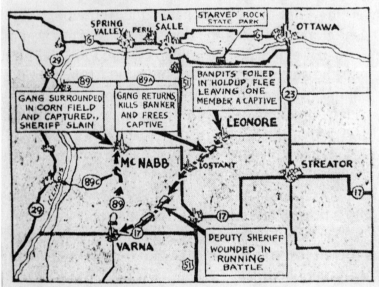

Newspapers recreated the bloody trail of the bank robbers in accounts following their dramatic flight and capture near **McNabb**.

toting citizens were slowly advancing toward the car.

Arthur Thielen, an unemployed plasterer and convicted narcotics peddler from upstate Rockford, was alone in the Willys Knight sedan waiting for his fellow conspirators. The other three thieves, Fred Gerner, John Hauff and gang leader Melvin Leist, had entered into the small bank before first light via the coal chute and lay in wait for the first worker to come in and open up. They had easily disconnected the building's crude burglar alarm, pocketed a small handful of pennies found in an unlocked drawer and unloaded the rifle which was always kept in plain view behind the teller's counter.

> **"Tell the law we still have the kid!"**
> John Hauff

Moving the rifle later proved to be the fatal flaw in what was to be a simple plan.

Bundy, who hurried to the bank after the phone warning, cautiously approached the front door while, inside, the three invaders raised their guns. The bank cashier cracked open the door only a few inches and he instantly noticed the bank's rifle was missing from its usual spot. As the robbers rushed toward him, Bundy slammed shut the thick door and ran shouting into the street for help. Behind the bank, getaway driver Thielen noticed a car was slowly creeping up behind him apparently in an attempt to block any escape. Panicking, he roared the engine to life and rammed the blocking car, leaving the others behind in the bank. Some of the advancing armed residents rushed forward at the sound of the crash and opened fire, slamming slugs into the sedan's engine and tires. It careened down the streets, only to break down seconds later at the edge of town. Shakened, Thielen scrambled out into a snow-covered cornfield.

In the unexpected confusion created by the vigilant committee's gunfire, the three stranded bandits escaped the bank and dodged more bullets as they ran into a nearby auto garage. Once inside, 16-year-old Norbert Naas, who was having his father's Model A Ford serviced, was taken hostage along with garage owner George Yusco by the desperate trio. Yusco was forced to drive one of his cars out into the streets while the terrified boy was held as a human shield on the running board.

The townspeople, realizing the car had escaped them, turned their attention toward capturing the getaway driver and ran to search the cornfield where his car had stopped. Bank officer Bundy and town supervisor Charles Seipp led the makeshift posse.

Miles from the growing gun battle, telephone operators, who were informed of the robbery before the first shots were fired in the streets of Leonore, began to alert county and state police departments throughout La Salle and surrounding counties, as well as informing farmers and residents in neighboring villages. Police and civilians raced across the countryside to set up roadblocks to trap the fleeing gang.

The bumbling bandits traveled but a few blocks when they forced garage owner Yusco to turn back into town. Frightened and screaming at their captives, they were nevertheless determined to find their missing conspirator before leaving the area. Young Naas was still on the running board, his arms and head held inside the car window.

In the interim, banker Bundy, Seipp and the other enraged citizens had pursued and easily captured the unarmed Thielen and were poking him in his back with their guns as they led him toward the road. Suddenly, the commandeered car roared back through the snowy streets directly at the startled group. Without warning, the bandits inside blasted their weapons at the posse. With their captive between them, Bundy was killed instantly, while Seipp felt his stomach being ripped open. Together, the two men slumped to the ground.

Thielen, untouched by the volley of shots, shouted, "Not me! Not Me!" as he ran to the car. The citizens returned the gunfire and wounded Thielen as he entered the escape vehicle. Just then, another slug smashed through the front windshield, grazing the forehead of the young Naas and tearing into his hand. The terrified boy didn't even realize that he had been shot until one of the robbers told him. A gun in his ribs, Yusco sped the car away from town. With wild terror in his eyes, Leist warned Thielen and the others that he would never be captured alive and that he would shoot anyone who tried to stop them.

Speeding across the countryside on ice-covered roads, the bandits decided that they should change cars. Waving their guns, they stopped a passing vehicle and forced themselves into it. At first, they left Yusco and the bleeding Haas on the cold roadside and drove away. Moments later, however, they came back and forced the boy into the car again, apparently thinking the youth would be better protection from police bullets.

To the south, Marshall County Sheriff Glenn "Mike" Axline, 32, had quickly organized a large posse with the help of Deputy Renis Brown. Leaving instructions with men at a roadblock near Magnolia, the officers went to search out the escaping gang. On the seat between the lawmen lay a fully loaded Thompson machine gun (the Marshall County Sheriff's Department purchased the deadly weapon much earlier from John "Trader Jack" Redshaw, the famous wheeler-dealer from Granville).

Traveling only a short distance from the roadblock, the police officers noticed a speeding car, suspiciously loaded with men, turn onto the road directly in front of them. Sheriff Axline sounded his car's siren. The auto in front pulled away. Chasing it, Axline fired a burst from the powerful Thompson at the targeted car. Several of the officer's bullets hit the already seriously wounded Thielen in the buttocks. As the thief screamed in pain, the hostage salesman slammed the car to a halt and jumped out, his hands in the air. The frightened man screamed, "Don't shoot! Don't shoot!" Running and slipping on ice, he dove behind a nearby tree and hid there.

This document recorded the state-induced deaths of the convicted **Leonore** bank robbery killers electrocuted in March 1935.

Thinking that this was a sign that the bandits were about to give up, Sheriff Axline stepped out from his car door, the smoking machine gun still in his hands. A split second later, the bandits fired several rounds out the back window. The shots killed Axline instantly and wounded Deputy Brown with a bullet that nearly tore off his arm. The gang rushed to the police car and tried to force the bleeding Brown to drive them; despite the guns aimed at his face, the deputy refused. Inexplicably, the bandits didn't kill the officer, but instead returned to their car again with Naas and the machine gun that they picked up off the snowy road. The leader Leist yelled, "Tell the law we still have the kid!" They drove away leaving the cold, shaking salesman, wounded deputy and the dead sheriff behind them.

Working in their farmhouse east of McNabb, Florence Ioerger and her mother only had to pick up their phone to hear the constant chatter on the line about the bungled robbery and gunplay that morning in nearby Leonore. However, they did notice the unusual number of cars rushing by their house, most of which were loaded with armed neighbors. So they were not overly concerned when an unfamiliar auto pulled into their yard. Looking out the window at the car and the several figures inside, Florence joked to her mother, "Maybe they're the bandits..." She walked out to see what the strangers wanted and to ask of any new developments of the holdup story.

In subsequent interviews, Florence said, "I invited them into the house, thinking they were some of the men who were hunting the bandits, and laughingly told them that I thought they might be the bandits. They said nothing in reply, and the nervous young boy with them apparently wasn't permitted to talk.

"Maybe they're the bandits..."
Florence Ioerger

"Just then the telephone rang and my mother started toward it. One of the men suddenly whipped out a gun and pointed it, shouting out, 'Don't answer that telephone!' "

Realizing that they were now hostages in their own home, the frightened mother and daughter were told to keep quiet and to stay away from the windows. It was then the women noticed the blood dripping onto the farmhouse floor from Thielen's and Naas' wounds. Concerned, Mrs. Ioerger began to dress the boy's hand injury while the criminals argued about their next move. One of them wanted to surrender, but Melvin Leist, machine gun hot in hand, swore to the others that he would never be captured.

Putnam County Sheriff Department officials, who gathered volunteers after the discovery of Sheriff Axline's murder, raced to the area of the Ioerger farm following reports the wanted car was sighted in the vicinity. Just before the posse approached the house, Hauff and Leist decided to try to escape on their own and left their cohorts, driving only a short distance before they oddly enough decided to abandon their car. From there, they made their way on foot through a snowy field outside McNabb.

Jacob Ioerger, working chores all morning, was stunned to find himself surrounded by armed men as he stepped out from his barn. Mistaken for one of the missing bandits, the farmer was almost shot by the agitated posse. Ioerger was completely unaware of the intruders who had invaded his

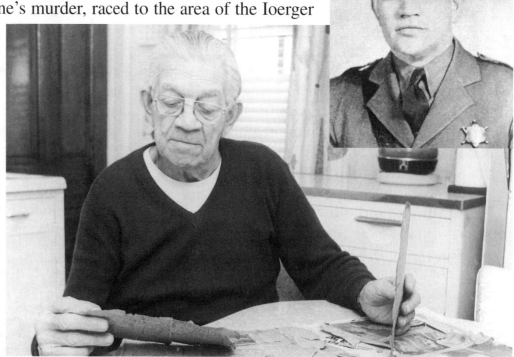

Joe Gromann, former Illinois State Trooper, reviews newspaper clippings in 1984 from one of his most infamous cases. As a young officer, **Gromann** was involved in a wild shoot-out which ended the day-long chase of the **Leonore** bank robbers.

home or that a massive manhunt was focused on his farm.

State Trooper Walter Bayer, backed by dozens of officers and civilians courageously entered the Ioerger house alone, clutching a gun in each hand. The two remaining bandits had gone upstairs, so the policeman took the mother, daughter and Naas outside to safety. Legend has it that another state trooper stepped inside the house with a live hand grenade, pulled the pin and yelled up the stairs for the robbers to give up or be blown up. Closer to the truth was the story that Bayer wanted to toss up a gas grenade but was talked out of it by the Ioergers, who didn't want their home damaged. Whatever happened, the cornered pair, Gerner and the bleeding Thielen, disappointed the heavily armed party by giving up without a fight.

With the remaining two criminals on foot and their general location known, the search was intensified throughout the rural area. A different country posse, composed of 30 to 35 high-strung farmers, loaded down with rifles, shotguns and pistols, kept watch on the outskirts around McNabb while police authorities circled the adjacent roads.

Illinois State troopers Joseph Gromann and Joseph Tutaj were the first to spot the fugitives, spying on them from a barn hayloft on the Charles Miller farm east of the village. The two policemen, each armed with a 30-30 repeating rifle, chased the running bandits into an open field. The officers were crouching about 300 yards away from them when Leist turned and fired a burst from the dead sheriff's stolen machine gun. The bullets peppered the snow at Gromann's feet and, as other officers and men approached from all directions, the two troopers fired back, sheltered only by piles of dried corn

State's Attorney Elmer Moran

stalks. They watched Leist and Hauff drop to their knees and begin to crawl through a barbed wire fence.

Gromann thought he wounded one of them, but Harry Reynolds, Streator's chief of police, later told the press, "They (the robbers) managed to crawl through the north fence as Gromann and Tutaj came on... then one of them (later identified as Leist) raised a 32-caliber revolver in his right hand and looked at us as we came up from the southwest. Believing he was going to fire at me, I covered him with my gun but didn't shoot. He then put the gun against his right temple and pulled the trigger."

Leist, shooting a hole into his head, kept his oath of freedom to himself.

Hauff, now clutching the machine gun, struggled to get loose of the spike-wire fence that held his clothes while police bullets whizzed by his head. The encircled man attempted to fire the Thompson, but it had jammed. He threw the gun down and waved a white handkerchief in surrender, screaming, "Don't shoot! Don't shoot!"

The chase had ended.

> "If you lift up this hood, you will see that I still have my smile."
>
> John Hauff

The next morning, as the statements of police and civilians were being recorded by various officials, La Salle County State's Attorney Elmer Mohan promised swift punishment to the three surviving gang members. Days later, while testimony continued to be recounted, Leonore's Charles Seipp died from his wounds at St. Mary's Hospital in Streator. His passing raised the death toll in the bloody crime to four. Cashier Bundy and Sheriff Axline were buried on the same day with each funeral drawing hundreds of mourners. In his moving eulogy, Rev. Roy Morgan spoke of the slain sheriff as a man who gave his life for friends and neighbors. He said, "If Mike could speak to us today, no words he could have chosen would be more appropriate. We are met here to pay tribute and to say farewell to a friend who fought the good fight and kept the faith to the end of the course."

The three prisoners, charged with the single crime of Charles Bundy's murder, were brought to trial on February 27, 1935. Standing before a packed courtroom, Prosecutor Mohan vented the rage of an entire county, "... they'll get the electric chair as long as I have anything to do with this case!" Labeling the trio as "man-killing outlaws," Mohan told the jury, "Gangsters and killers of their type are not for the penitentiaries. There is only one thing that they fear —death— for death means the end for them! If you will serve notice on all other criminals by returning a death verdict in this case, you will be cooperating with the ends of the anticrime movement!"

Defendants Gerner and Thielen pleaded not guilty to the murder charge (their attorneys claimed that the dead ringleader, Leist, was the only man who could be blamed for Bundy's death) while Hauff fully confessed his guilt before the court. Hauff, who stood in the shadow of the electric chair, said that he was "safe in Christ Jesus." Within the confines of the La Salle County jailhouse in Ottawa, the doomed prisoner claimed to have "triumphed over Satan," with the help of a local Baptist minister. He told reporters he was reborn with God and had peace in his heart. He prayed constantly. From his cramped cell, Hauff wrote to his wife: "The outcome doesn't worry me in the least as far as I'm concerned. I've placed myself unreservedly in God's care and (I will) accept the judgement given."

The county's verdict came swiftly as Mohan had promised. Following almost two weeks of testimony, the 12 jury members decreed death; the judge concurred. On March 18, Judge Robert E. Larking pronounced their sentences. He told the crowded assembly, "The killing of Charles Bundy was unnecessarily willful, wanton and deliberate. There was no lack of intelligence, no intoxication, no uncontrollable passion. It will be the sentence of this court that the death penalty shall be inflicted on the 11th day of April, 1935 within the walls of the Illinois State Penitentiary at Joliet."

Family members of the condemned men wept and cried aloud as the judge spoke. Gerner's sister fainted to the floor and had to be carried from the courtroom. The three prisoners themselves, however, took the verdict with little visible emotion.

The pronouncement of the three death sentences marked the first time in more than 40 years that a La Salle County judge had imposed such penalties. The last court-ordered execution took the life of 22-year-old Charles Ford of Ottawa on the morning of May 9, 1891. The young man, who claimed innocence to the very end, was hung in the county's jailyard for the brutal murder of David Moore, a traveling salesman in

Ottawa during the summer of 1890. Ford had beaten Moore to death after a woman accomplice lured the salesman to Ottawa's Allen Park to attempt a robbery. Although hundreds were drawn to the scene of the hanging, only a handful of witnesses actually viewed the execution. Guards armed with high-powered rifles maintained a vigil atop high boarded fences that shielded the public from the hand-crafted scaffold. With the noose tight around his neck, Ford dropped to his death while many of the witnesses whispered prayers.

Unlike modern day justice in the 1990s, in 1935 the standard appeal process only backed up the execution date by one month to May 10. Further appeals taken directly to Illinois Governor Henry Horner for reprieves were quickly rejected. Shortly after midnight that morning, each of the three men had their heads shaven and their trousers split up the leg. Gerner and Thielen rejected their final meal, while Hauff, apparently at peace with his fate, reportedly "ate heartily on a sumptuous chicken dinner."

Gerner, his face hidden under a black hood, was the first to be led into the glass enclosed chamber which held the death chair. Among the crowd of 150 witnesses were the brothers of the slain Sheriff Axline. None of the prisoners' relatives were allowed to witness the executions. Asking forgiveness from God and the families of the slain men, Gerner sat up straight and rock steady as thousands of volts of electricity surged between the metal plates strapped to his body. He was pronounced dead at 1:04 a.m. by the prison physician. In the next 18 minutes, both Hauff and Thielen, still suffering from their serious bullet wounds, were also electrocuted and each pronounced dead.

The final chapter of the Leonore bank robbery, a crime that took seven lives and netted seven pennies, were penned by the late Rev. P. B. Chenault of La Salle in a small booklet entitled, "How God Dealt with a Bank Robber." Chenault, who had been Hauff's spiritual counsel during the final days of his life, documented the prisoner's religious awakening to his last minute. In the pamphlet, the minister wrote that Hauff's brave last words were, "If you lift up this hood, you will see that I still have my smile..."

Regarded as one of the most spectacular high school football fields in the midwest and, quite possibly the country, **Howard Fellows Stadium** serves as the home field of the **La Salle-Peru High School** Cavalier football team. The stadium was originally constructed in 1937 and received a multimillion dollar facelift in 1996. L-P school commencement ceremonies are also often held each spring in the sports facility.

Slicing through a nearly frozen
Illinois River, a tug with loaded
barges passes under one of the area's
many bridges.

SHIPYARD ON THE PRAIRIE

The year was 1942.

The vast shipyard was an explosion of activity 24 hours a day. Sparks from hundreds of arc-welding rods flew into the open air like fireworks as workers fused together massive pieces of steel. Women and men, an astounding 11,000 of them, toiled side-by-side at a furious pace. World War II had been ripping the planet and its people apart for years and the U.S. Navy demanded more vessels for action on two fronts. Shipbuilding facilities on both coasts had been pushed beyond their limits and the real fear was that they were vulnerable from sea attack. Naval authorities pressed for inland manufacturing plants that would be safe from any possible air or sea raids. Pearl Harbor had changed America forever. Americans would not lose this war. So to the heart of the Midwest, the shipbuilders came.

Pressed for a new kind of ocean-going ship which would be capable of delivering men, machines and materials with surprising speed to invasion beaches rather than regular ports, U.S. Naval engineers quickly designed an innovative flat-bottom ship. The new vessel, dubbed Landing Ship Tank or LST, was envisioned with a shallow draft and huge carrying capacity to conduct amphibious warfare. The blueprints called for the new ship to feature giant bow doors and ramps to assist in the rapid unloading of any cargo. Though it was not expected to be a fighting ship, the LST would also be outfitted with a battery of

The Illinois prairie stretches flat in the background of this aerial photograph showing the once famous **Senica** LST shipyard. Tens of thousands of dedicated men and women worked frantically day and night to produce Landing Ship Tanks, the workhorse of the United States Navy fleet during the last fright-filled days of World War II.

armaments for the protection of craft and crew. The Navy's central design and general procurement agent, Gibbs and Cox, Inc. of New York, was delegated the responsibility of overseeing the flow of materials to all 18 of the nations's shipbuilding yards selected for LST construction.

Carved out of the banks of the Illinois River, Seneca was a quiet farm community of under 1,500. The village was far removed from the stark horrors of combat, but the patriotic townpeoples' minds and souls were committed to the frantic ongoing American war effort. So the residents were both elated and proud when the announcement came that the Chicago Iron and Bridge Company, under the auspices and financial support of the Naval Department, was to build a vital shipyard there. Merle J. Trees, vice-president of the Chicago company, confirmed the news with the disclosure that nearly $7 million had been earmarked for the yard's initial construction and support housing costs.

157 LSTs were built and delivered on schedule to the Navy from out of the cornfield shipyard.

The reasons why Seneca was selected for this wartime mission were varied and many. The main trunk line of the Rock Island Line Railroad and the heavily-traveled State Route 6 highway artery cut through the town near the river. Massive amounts of needed electricity was available from the nearby main power line of the Northern Illinois Power Company. Its close proximity to the Great Lakes and therefore, an abundance of raw materials, was an important factor. Also, the chosen site on the north bank featured a convenient steep slope ideally suited for ship launching purposes and, perhaps most important of all, the shoreline was on a solid base of rigid sandstone rock.

Construction was started in April 1942 as a few giant Caterpillar tractors and a small army of men began the grading and digging of the former cornfield. Some 300,000 cubic yards of rich, black dirt 30 inches deep were scraped off of the 200-acre site, leaving a nearly flat area of solid sandstone. Site manager Donald Leach also supervised the digging of three deep wells which eventually supplied the operations with nearly a half million gallons of water daily during peak periods. As the first few weeks and months passed, a seemingly endless caravan of trucks, equipment and manpower poured into the village. Virtually overnight, the peacefulness of tiny Seneca was replaced by the constant and thunderous din of a thousand hammers and saws building the support facilities, housing and the actual shipyard.

And the people came. By the thousands, workers of all ages traveled from every corner of the country in the hope of securing a job. They rolled into town, many with their life possessions strapped to the top of their jalopies. The newcomers quickly overran the town's small restaurants and stores as well as putting tremendous stress on the village's existing services. Realizing the importance of their homefront mission, Seneca residents welcomed the new neighbors with warm hospitality. In the first few weeks of the work invasion many of the villagers invited complete strangers into their homes for temporary shelter and meals while buildings and barracks were literally pounded together overnight.

To insure that the Seneca yard would function at the highest level of efficiency, a unique "task system" was developed as it became apparent that existing shipbuilding methods would have to be discarded. The new LSTs would be 90 percent completed on land, unlike past shipbuilding practices. That method reduced delays and ultimately made it possible to send the craft out to sea (via the Illinois and Mississippi Rivers) a mere 10 days after launching. The new system trained hundreds of crews to perform their very specialized work on the ships quickly as the ships slowly

Typical of their mission to convey precious manpower and supplies to the front lines, **LST**s were crammed with an astounding amount of men and materials.

moved from berth to berth heading toward the river. Upon completion of its task, a crew would jump from ship to ship to perform the same work. Daily reports documented the 387 tasks, some involving more than 1,100 complex operations, which were required to complete one LST. Continuous reviews of these reports would constantly adjust the construction schedule on Seneca's quarter-mile long "assembly line."

Frank Volk of La Salle was working as a short-order cook in a small restaurant when he first learned of the work opportunities at the new shipyard. He soon joined in the confusion of the growing industrial complex with several other friends and neighbors who were hired as unskilled laborers. "I worked mostly as a 'chipper' preparing the steel before it was welded together," Volk said, adding, "... it was a good job to have at that time." The work week consisted of six nine-hour

On his ship, the LST 1138, my father, **Jim Stout** of Galesburg, sailed from the shipyards at **Senica** to the mainland of Japan during the final days of WWII. President Harry Truman's decision to use atomic weapons in the summer of 1945 cancelled plans for a bloody invasion of the enemy's home islands. The LST, many of which were constructed in **Senica**, would have played a major role in such an massive amphibious attack.

days with the pay rate of time and a half for hours after 40, bringing the average hours up to 61 after dinner/ lunch breaks. Wages ranged from 83 cents per hour for basic unskilled labor to $1.20 per hour for trained craftsmen and mechanics. For night work, the pay scale was increased five cents per hour. Near the end of the shipyard's short lifespan, some of the more highly skilled workers were paid at piece rate, boosting some paychecks to a then astounding $200 a week. The start times for each shift were staggered somewhat for various workers in order that traffic in and about the yard was spread out over an hour or two. The shipyard labor force was unionized and relationships between management and the craft workers were very good. Although the majority of the Senica employees joined the American Federation of Labor Union without question, there were those who did object to payment of the required union dues. No serious conflicts involving the union organization were ever recorded. Volk's favorite memory from that time was the day he actually got to ride on one of the LSTs as it slid into the Illinois River. "It bobbed up and down in the water like a bathtub," he laughed, commenting on the flat bottom of the ships.

  The LSTs built in Seneca were hailed by many officers as the "best ships in the fleet." The 50-foot wide ship had three decks and was 327-feet long with a height of 28-feet. The tank or third deck was a cavernous compartment specially constructed to discharge possible cargo or troops from its built-in ramp directly onto any beach. With these facilities, the LST could berth and transport as many as 1,000 troops, though admittedly that number would create near-suffocating conditions. From its cramped engine room, the ship was powered by two 900-horsepower diesel engines along with three huge generators for its electrical needs.

Even though the birth of the shipyard created many problems for the little village, the people of Seneca and the newcomers worked together to solve each one, often with amazing ingenuity. Shipbuilding crews worked at a feverous pitch and launched their first ship, the LST 197, on schedule on Dec. 13, 1942. Cheering crowds lined the banks of the Illinois River to watch as the vessel, christened with a broken bottle of champagne, was released sideways down a 327-foot slide. Reaching a speed of almost 30 miles per hour, the ship created a huge wake that scattered onlookers as large waves splashed onto the shore. The LST 197 was rapidly completed in the water and commissioned into Navy hands on Jan. 20, 1943. Later

that year, as the Seneca workers finetuned their skills, ships were finished in half the time it took to build the first one. Launchings, which were considered the most influential of morale-builders, soon increased to five or six ships per month. Accompanied by music and speeches by visiting dignitaries or celebrities (movie star Cesar Romero participated in one launching), each ceremony was a reminder to the labor force of the importance of their work. A peak number of 11,000 employees was reached in 1944 and more than

Although often ridiculed for its slow speed and tubby appearance, the **Seneca**-built LST was ultimately proven to be one of America's most valuable weapons in WWII.

27,000 different people worked at the Seneca works during its three-year lifespan. In fact, at the peak of the wartime boom in the small village, Navy officials announced that "Construction of LST's such as those built at Seneca is the hottest job in the country now!"

As the LSTs slowly made their way on to war, the ship's high profile and slow speed invited various nicknames for the Navy's unglamorous (if not down-right ugly) workhorses. Sailors called them "Large Slow Target" or "Large Stranded Target" or even "Last Ship (to) Tokyo." Indeed, it took the LSTs a long time to get anywhere. For example, it took a week for an LST to reach the Aleutians from San Francisco, a voyage which took most U.S. vessels of that time a mere three days. However, their wartime performance was so efficient that the LST soon became one of the most valuable vessels in coastal invasion missions. Hundreds were used in such notable battles as Normandy, Iwo Jima and Okinawa to name just a few.

> ## "It was a good job to have at that time."
> ### Frank Volk

My father, James F. Stout, Jr., of Galesburg, Illinois was a high school senior in 1944. Along with his fellow classmates (as well as most other young American boys of that era), he was desperate to enlist and fight for his country in the great World War. At the age of 17 years old, he was too young to sign up without his parent's permission and, upon graduating he joined the Navy with their blessing. Following boot camp at Great Lakes Naval Training Center and additional training at bases in Virginia and Florida, my Dad was one of 103 enlisted sailors who reported aboard the newly launched LST 1138 on April 18, 1945. A river-experienced ferry crew trained officers and crew during the shakedown cruise down the Illinois and Mississippi Rivers. After more repairs and alterations were completed at harbors near New Orleans and along the coast of Alabama, the new ship was loaded with 928 tons of cased ammunition, rockets and pyrotechnic shells, as well as tons of other vital materials. The vessel and crew were then ordered to Pearl Harbor via the Panama Canal for duty in the Pacific Operating Areas. After only a few months of delivering supplies and ammunition in and around the Philippine Islands and other parts of the mid-Pacific Ocean, the LST 1138 joined a huge floating armada making frantic preparations for the expected bloody invasion of the

main island of Japan. "In August 1945, we were only a few hundred miles off the coast of Japan when we learned of the atomic bomb attacks and the surrender," my Dad recalled, adding "our ship was then ordered to Wakayama, Honshu, Japan." During the next several weeks in Japan, the LST 1138 also moved and anchored near Nagasaki, the city nearly destroyed in the second atomic bomb raid. Referring to the blast which killed 40,000 people, "Big boom! Big Boom!," was the only English spoken by the Japanese, according to my father's remembrances from that time more than 50 years ago. He stayed with the same ship until his discharge in the summer of 1946. The Seneca-made LST 1138 continued in Naval service and actually earned multiple battle stars from action off and on the shores of Korea during the early 1950s.

All in all, 157 LSTs were built and delivered on schedule to the Navy out of the cornfield shipyard. The last ship, the USS LST 1152, splashed into the Illinois River on June 8, 1945. Alice Kline of Utica, then an employee of the shipyard's housing authority and wife to Alexander Kline, Seneca's electrical maintenance superintendent, smashed the ceremonial champagne bottle across her bow. Interviewed in the La Salle Daily News-Tribune 50 years later, Kline said, "I can remember being a little bit nervous about giving a speech. It was festive because they had completed the contract." Besides the honor of heading the final ceremony, Mrs. Kline was also presented with a commemorative bottle of champagne in an inscribed wooden box. It is a treasured keepsake that she continues to display in her home to this day.

As with all government projects, recordkeepers compiled hundreds of various facts and figures from the closing shipyard which included:

- ◆Seneca shipbuilders purchased more than $9 million in U.S. War Bonds.

- ◆The yard's cafeteria served more than 6 million meals.

- ◆More than 20,000 Navy officers and crew were required to man all the Seneca ships.

- ◆39 gallons of champagne were used for the regular christenings.

- ◆More than $82 million was paid out to Seneca workers using more than 1,200,000 paychecks.

- ◆Placing all of the Seneca LSTs end to end would make a steel wall 10 miles in length.

- ◆Moving all the 157 ships through the yard and into the water was equivalent to moving one ship 37 miles.

After the launching of the last constructed LST, the shipyard was slowly abandoned and leased out to various businesses over the years. On April 26, 1974, the acreage was purchased from the federal government for $363,000 by the Seneca Port Authority for use as an industrial park. There is little left at the site to remind anyone of the once massive work area. Now, in the mid-1990s, hundreds of World War II Navy veterans hold various regular reunions to preserve the memory of their LST adventures, but many are disappointed that nothing remains from the "prairie shipyard." The location is now used as a staging and loading area for grain barges floating on the muddy Illinois River.

In the 1980s, efforts were begun to purchase a Seneca-built LST which had been sold overseas and return it back to the abandoned shipyard site as the mainstay of a memorial park and museum. Although much time and effort was put into the project by former sailors from all over the country, the plan collapsed as the Republic of China realized that the new "Seneca Navy" would not be able to raise the $1.3 million to pilot the ship back to its point of origin. The failure to secure the boat was a major disappointment to many LST veterans who attend Navy reunions regularly across the nation. In 1973, the Chicago Bridge and Iron Company donated a scale model of an LST ship to the La Salle County Historical Museum in Utica. The modest display salutes the underpraised work of those men and women who helped to win the world war from their own backyard.

An adventurous hiker soaks in a shower of rainwater cascading from the standstone canyon walls inside **Starved Rock State Park**.